Doctor Arne

Dr Arne

Doctor Arne

by
HUBERT LANGLEY

CAMBRIDGE
AT THE UNIVERSITY PRESS
1938

CAMBRIDGE
UNIVERSITY PRESS

University Printing House, Cambridge CB2 8BS, United Kingdom

Cambridge University Press is part of the University of Cambridge.

It furthers the University's mission by disseminating knowledge in the pursuit of education, learning and research at the highest international levels of excellence.

www.cambridge.org
Information on this title: www.cambridge.org/9781107437869

© Cambridge University Press 1938

This publication is in copyright. Subject to statutory exception and to the provisions of relevant collective licensing agreements, no reproduction of any part may take place without the written permission of Cambridge University Press.

First published 1938
First paperback edition 2014

A catalogue record for this publication is available from the British Library

ISBN 978-1-107-43786-9 Paperback

Cambridge University Press has no responsibility for the persistence or accuracy of URLs for external or third-party internet websites referred to in this publication, and does not guarantee that any content on such websites is, or will remain, accurate or appropriate.

CONTENTS

PREFACE		page vii
CHAPTER I.	Handel in England	1
II.	Then and Now	4
III.	The Evidence of Dr Burney	9
IV.	The Arne Family	12
V.	*Comus* and *The Judgment of Paris*	19
VI.	*The Masque of Alfred* and "Rule, Britannia!"	26
VII.	Shakespeare and Dublin	33
VIII.	The Songs	42
IX.	Mrs Arne	53
X.	Operas and Ballad Operas	64
XI.	*The Fairy Prince*—Death and Commemoration	75
XII.	*Judith*	88
XIII.	Requiescat—et Resurgat	97
APPENDIX A.	Extant works of Arne	107
APPENDIX B.	Modern editions of Arne's works	110
BIBLIOGRAPHY		114
INDEX		115

PLATES

DR ARNE *Frontispiece*
From a drawing by BARTOLOZZI

SUSANNAH MARIA CIBBER *facing page* 16
After T. HUDSON. (By courtesy of Messrs Hutchinson.)

MUSICAL EXAMPLES

1. From the song "Not on beds of fading flow'rs" (*Comus*).   21
2. From the overture to *The Judgment of Paris*.   24
3. Introduction to the song "Rule, Britannia!". (*The Masque of Alfred*).   29
4. From the song "Sleep, gentle Cherub" (*Judith*).   93
5, 6. From the chorus "Here, sons of Jacob" (*Judith*).   95, 96
7, 8. From the dirge "*Libera me*".   99, 100

PREFACE

My excuse for writing about Dr Arne's music is that no other book on the same subject exists at all. The late Dr W. H. Cummings in his helpful *Dr Arne and "Rule, Britannia!"* has given valuable hints as to where much of Arne's best music is to be found, but he has concentrated chiefly on "Rule, Britannia!" and many of his pages are devoted to the correspondence with David Garrick.

Most of the facts known about Arne's life can be read in Grove's *Dictionary of Music* and the article in the *Dictionary of National Biography*, but unless we are acquainted with his music he himself can be of very little interest to us, and in my humble plea for Dr Arne my only wish has been to bring to the notice of musicians and publishers those that I consider the most important works of a composer who was in his own day a very great figure in English music.

Some day perhaps a scholarly work, which will include a thorough examination of Arne's music from a more technical point of view, will be undertaken by a writer fully qualified to do so. In the meantime if this little book can be of any use in assisting others, who may share my enthusiasm, to investigate the subject further, or, better still, to help with the publication of the music, its object will have been satisfactorily achieved.

HUBERT LANGLEY

11 *Belgrave Road*
London, S.W.
November 1938

Chapter I

HANDEL IN ENGLAND

The fact that Handel should have chosen to establish himself in England for life, though it conferred innumerable and obvious blessings on his adopted country, has had two decided disadvantages. The more serious and far-reaching of these is that his music has, ever since his death, been less widely known in other lands than that of any other composer approaching him in eminence. For whereas it has always been the custom of English people to go abroad to hear music, and to bring home musical ideas, yet foreign musicians have never been greatly concerned with what is happening in our island, except those who have come over here to increase their own reputations, and to take back our money. The unrestrained enthusiasm for Handel which prevailed in England from the beginning of the reign of George III until the closing years of the nineteenth century left little or no impression on the minds and tastes of the leaders of musical fashion on the Continent. Even Haydn expressed astonishment at the mighty chorus from *Joshua*, on hearing it for the first time at one of the annual commemoration concerts at Westminster Abbey, a fact that suggests that Handel's music was not at that time well known in Austria.

It is, however, with the second regrettable result of Handel's residence in England that we are more particularly concerned when considering the merit and reputation of his English contemporaries.

The popularity of Handel in England has probably no parallel in the whole history of music. When caprice and faction, after wrecking his fortunes and ruining his health, had finally surrendered to his unconquerable spirit and incorruptible mind, the English nation set up an altar to him at which they worshipped with unswerving devotion for over a hundred years. His music invaded their religious observances, their ceremonial occasions, and the intimate gatherings in their homes.

Monster choral societies were formed for the purpose of singing his oratorios, and festivals inaugurated for the performance of his music in gigantic concert halls, which were, however, scarcely large enough to hold the multitudes which flocked to them from end to end of the United Kingdom. Even the Mendelssohn fever at the height of its rage was unable seriously to shake Handel's supremacy, and it is not wonderful that in the blaze of that great sun all the lesser lights were extinguished, which, before that sun had reached its full meridian, had burnt with no faint ray.

The honours thus paid to Handel, which were no more than his due, had one unfortunate result: during his lifetime there were native English composers of genius, whose styles were largely modelled on his, but who nevertheless had the originality to produce much that is good, and something that is great. Of this store of beautiful music hardly anything remains in any form that is of practical use in concerts or the theatre. The most important works of Arne, Boyce, and Greene are out of print, and the musical public knows nothing of them, save only an occasional song, sonata or anthem which has been rescued as a brand from the burning.

Had Handel not lived at the same time, and entirely overshadowed them, it is fairly safe to assert that their works would have survived, and been in constant request at the present day; and the glory of their once so illustrious names would have remained undimmed. Among those names the most conspicuous and most justly celebrated is Thomas Augustine Arne.

Chapter II

THEN AND NOW

The rise and decline of any great reputation affords an interesting if somewhat melancholy study, but if it chances that that reputation should enjoy a second spring, the revival is apt to be attended by illuminating incidents.

There is a well-known joke in theatrical circles that during the long run of *The Beggar's Opera* at Hammersmith, 1920–3, the officers of the Inland Revenue, hopefully thinking that they had "got a good thing", sent to the theatre an income-tax form to be filled up by the poet Gay, who had died in the reign of George II. It is not so well known that, just before a revival of Arne's music to *Comus* in 1922, a firm of photographers in Bond Street invited Dr Arne to sit for them; but this actually happened. One might reasonably have hoped that even if all his other works were irretrievably lost, the name of the composer of "Rule, Britannia!" would still be known throughout the Empire, but alas! that is very far from being the case, and the blame must rest not on the ignorance of the photographers, but on the apathy and negligence of the musicians who have omitted to keep his memory green, and who do not, even once in each year, give us an opportunity of hearing our great national song in the form in which it was composed. The familiar version, condensed and incorrect both as regards music and words, is a mere travesty in which the grandeur and dignity of the original have no part. But we will leave "Rule, Britannia!" to a later chapter, and turn our attention to its composer.

The stories of Handel and Arne begin in much the same way, but there the resemblance ends, for Handel was a mental and spiritual phenomenon such as occurs but a few times in history, whereas it is only as a musician that Arne is of any interest at all. Nevertheless the former as an infant, and the latter as a boy, had much the same difficulties to contend with, and both overcame them. There were no traces of music in any of their ancestors, no musical influences in their homes; both were destined to the law by fathers who strongly disapproved of their early musical inclinations, but who were both wise enough, when they had once discovered that these symptoms were too strong to be suppressed, to allow their sons to pursue the path which was to lead to eternal fame; and while Handel tinkled in an attic on a muffled spinet, Arne did his best on a "miserable cracked flute" at Eton.

Yes, Arne was at Eton, but, as we are told nothing about his schooldays beyond the fact that his companions did not care for his fluting, it seems probable that the little flute player himself was not much appreciated, and that the old instrument was his only friend. Yet who knows whether some of the songs which were soon to be sung all over England

and Ireland, many of which delight us still, were not directly descended from the rather painful sounds which came from that old flute? Perhaps even now it might be allowed to some young Etonian wandering across the school yard at fairy time to hear the strains of the flute floating around, while the holy Henry,* himself the composer of a fine Sanctus, smiles indulgently from his pedestal as he listens to the first attempts of the little boy, whose portrait he knows is hanging in the gallery of illustrious Etonians, the only representative of music, among soldiers, statesmen, prelates and writers.

Eton has reason to be proud of Arne. She had never before nurtured a musical genius, and she had to wait another century and a half for Hubert Parry, whose future fame, curiously enough, seems likely to rest on another, though totally dissimilar, national song, his setting of another eighteenth-century poem.†

But whether or not Dr Arne and his work are known and valued by the uneducated musician, no student of musical history can deny that he is one of the most prominent figures in English music, for during his own lifetime his works enjoyed a greater success and popularity than was accorded to those of any other English composer, even Purcell, and that in an age of considerable taste, and at a time when Handel's imposing procession of oratorios was en-

* King Henry VI.
† Blake's "Jerusalem".

gaging the attention of all the best critics. His early successes in Dublin were almost equal to the furore created by Handel in that city, and the enthusiasm with which *Comus* was received fell little short of that which greeted the first performance of *Messiah*. It must be remembered, however, that Arne had on that occasion the best possible advance publicity agent in his sister, Susannah, the renowned Mrs Cibber, whose singing of "He was despised" had caused the Dean of Down, good Dr Delany, to rise up before the whole assembly and absolve her of all her sins, past, present and to come. This talented lady acted just as well as she sang, and David Garrick declared when she died that "Tragedy expired with her".

Again it is impossible to acquire any very extensive knowledge of the eighteenth century without forming some sort of acquaintance with Doctor Arne. The greater part of his work was done for the theatre, and theatrical history between the years 1730 and 1780 is to a great extent the story of Arne, his friends and his associates. His sister, Susannah, was married to the worthless son of Colley Cibber, poet laureate, actor and writer of comedies; Arne was himself associated with David Garrick at Drury Lane Theatre; his masques were acted by Quin and Kitty Clive, and his songs sung by Beard, the famous tenor.

There are constant references to him in contemporary literature. The vitriolic Churchill hurls abuse at him in *The Rosciad* for no worse a crime than that of introducing Italian singers, *castrati* and all that fry, on to the English stage; Smollett in *Roderick Random* alludes to what he terms a fashionable air, which proves to be the lovely "Would you taste the noontide air?" from *Comus*; there is also a reference in *She Stoops to Conquer* to "Water parted from the sea", one of the very few of Arne's songs whose popularity has never quite faded; but perhaps the most convincing evidence of his great reputation, and of the esteem in which he was held even so late as 1816, is to be found in Keats's Epistle to Charles Cowden Clarke. The poet, excusing himself for his bad verses, tells his friend that he has recently been out of reach of any inspiring influences, and says:

> But many days have past since last my heart
> Was warm'd luxuriously by divine Mozart,
> By Arne delighted, or by Handel madden'd,
> Or by the song of Erin pierced and sadden'd.

Arne was still in great company!

Chapter III

THE EVIDENCE OF DR BURNEY

Any statement or opinion advanced by the learned Dr Burney is entitled to our attention and respect. He was himself a competent composer, a man of great erudition and experience, and was intimately acquainted with everyone in England distinguished in literature and the arts.

In the year 1744 he was a pupil of Arne, who offered to teach him for a consideration, but who, when the bargain had been struck, discovered that the duties of educating even so apt a scholar as Burney were not congenial to his own volatile nature, and was only too ready to be relieved of the burden by Fulk Greville who, wishing for the services of Burney as performer and teacher, bought him from Arne for the sum of three hundred pounds.

We know little of the relations between them in later years, but this was not a promising start, and the further manifestations of Arne's nature were not such as to inspire great enthusiasm in a man of Burney's moral integrity and exemplary character.

Burney's estimate of Arne's music is on the whole very high and very just, but he is unable to resist the temptation of comparing him unfavourably with Handel, which is neither fair nor reasonable;

and this is all the more exasperating, for in so doing he has flatly contradicted himself.

His first reference to Arne in the *History of Music* is at the head of a list of composers whose utmost attempts, he says, were no more than a humble and timid imitation of Handel's style. Later we are rather astonished at being told that "Arne was never a close imitator of Handel", and that he had real genius.

In this connection Fétis also is worth quoting, who disliked all things English, and repaid Burney's taunts upon French music by sneering at the English composers. He says that "*Arne eut du moins le mérite d'y mettre un cachet particulier, et de ne point se borner comme tous les compositeurs anglais de cette époque, à imiter Purcell ou Handel.*"

Again the good doctor creates considerable confusion in our minds, when he treats of Arne's operas in the Italian style. He gives us what appear to be two diametrically opposite opinions. Accounting for the failure of the opera *Olimpiade*, he tells us that "Arne had kept bad company: he had written for vulgar singers and hearers too long to be able to comport himself properly at the opera-house, in the first circle of taste and fashion. The common playhouse and ballad passages, which occurred in almost every air in his opera made the audience wonder how they got there." But a very few pages further on we read that "In 1762 Arne quitted the former style of melody, in which he had so well set *Comus*, and furnished Vauxhall and the whole kingdom with such songs as had improved and polished national taste, and when he set Metastasio's opera *Artaxerxes* he crowded the airs with all the Italian divisions and difficulties which had ever been heard at the opera."

It is difficult here to see exactly what Burney meant. There seems to be no pleasing him, for were not the "common ballad passages" the same as those which furnished Vauxhall, and was not *Comus* composed for the playhouse?

But when all this has been said and allowed for, it is not difficult for us to see that Burney prized the music of Arne very highly, and acknowledged his genius with no inconsiderable praise. He tells us a second time that the music of *Comus* and the songs composed for Vauxhall form an era in English music, and affected our national taste; he reminds us that Arne had a new style of his own, and in conclusion draws a comparison between him and Purcell, wherein he gives to the earlier composer the palm for fertility of ideas, grandeur of thought, and greater resources, yet in secular music he considers that Arne surpassed Purcell in ease, grace and variety.

We have called Dr Burney into the court because any attempt to reinstate a fallen idol is too frequently viewed with suspicion by the uninstructed, and the evidence of one of the greatest scholars of his age cannot be treated with disdain.

Chapter IV

THE ARNE FAMILY

Thomas Arne was born in March 1710 (the exact date is uncertain), and was baptised in the Church of St Paul's, Covent Garden, on May 28th of that year. His father's name was also Thomas, and his mother before her marriage was Anne Wheeler, whom Dr Burney describes as a bigoted Roman Catholic. At his baptism young Arne received only the one name, and it is probable that owing to his mother's influence he was brought up as a member of the Roman Catholic Church, and adopted his second name, Augustine, at his confirmation.

Thomas was born at his father's house in King Street, Covent Garden, now number 34, but in 1710 it was known as the "Crown and Cushion". This house had acquired temporary fame before the composer's birth, for it was there that the North American chieftains resided on their visit to London which caused so great a sensation. They came as emissaries to Queen Anne to seek her aid against the French in Canada, and were billeted on Thomas Arne, senior.

The elder Arne was by trade an upholsterer and coffin-maker, and rather a gruesome story is told of how young Thomas was once found by Michael Festing practising the fiddle with the music propped up on a coffin. Festing observed that he would not care to use the coffin as a music desk as he would always be imagining that a corpse was inside, whereupon Arne raised the lid, and showed that the coffin did in very truth contain a corpse.

It cannot be claimed for the family of Arne that it was either ancient or honourable. The first known bearer of the name was the composer's grandfather, Thomas Arne, who married Mary Thursfield in 1680, died in 1713 in the Marshalsea debtor's prison, and was buried in the graveyard of St Paul's, Covent Garden. His son Thomas, the father of the composer, evidently managed his business more successfully and had a keen eye to the main chance, for, being once persuaded that his children would prosper in the theatre, he not only withdrew his objections to their following their own natural inclinations, but speculated in music himself in a manner very far from reputable. He arranged a dramatic version of *Acis and Galatea* at the Haymarket Theatre without consulting Handel or asking his permission to do so; and so for the first time was this most perfect rural idyll acted on the stage, a method of performance which was in all probability directly contrary to the composer's wishes.

Of the composer's uncle, Edward Arne, a most horrific tale is told. He was done to death in a terrible manner in the Fleet prison. It appears that in 1725, "while he was in the tap-house of the prison and behaving himself quietly he was suddenly seized by one James Barnes, agent for John Huggins, the Warden of the Fleet, and forced into a dungeon, so damp that the drops hung upon the walls. In this place he was locked up and never once permitted to go out. But by an accident on a Sunday, the door being opened, he ran into the parlour adjoining the chapel during the time of Divine Service; he had no covering for his body but the feathers of a bed into which he had crept to defend himself from the cold, and the feathers stuck and were clotted upon him by his own excrements and the dirt which covered his skin. He was seized and carried back to the dungeon, where from cold and want of food he lost his senses and died." John Huggins was tried for murder but acquitted; his agent Barnes fled beyond the sea to avoid being brought to trial.

Such was the family into which the illustrious song-writer and his accomplished sister were born. There is nothing to create the impression that the children of the house of Arne were likely to be reared in wisdom and probity, and we ought not to be too greatly disappointed when we find that their moral reputation left something to be desired, and that the composer's son Michael, twice beggared by his insane efforts to find the Philosopher's Stone, was shut up for a time in Dublin prison from which he had to be rescued by his friends.

Susannah Maria Arne, who was her brother's junior by four years, became one of the greatest personalities of the eighteenth-century stage, and also achieved notoriety as the principal of a famous *cause célèbre.* At the age of twenty, she was married,

THE ARNE FAMILY 15

very much against her will, to Theophilus Cibber, an actor of extravagant and drunken habits. Four years later Cibber had to fly the country in order to be out of the way of his creditors. When he returned he brought an action against a Mr Sloper for criminal conversation with his wife. The general impression was that he had deliberately thrown her in Sloper's way with a view to obtaining damages. In this he was disappointed, for though he claimed damages to the amount of £5000, the jury awarded him only £5, thus expressing their opinion of his connivance. In the following year, however, he brought another action asking for £10,000. This time he was given £500. Susannah never returned to him, and after spending a considerable portion of his life in prison he was shipwrecked and drowned in the Irish Sea. His wife lived with Sloper until her death in 1766, and to judge from passages in her letters to David Garrick it is evident that their union was a happy one. She was buried in the cloisters of Westminster Abbey.

Mrs Cibber, to use the name by which she is best known, has a position almost unique in stage history. From the accounts of all the best authorities, which include Quin and Garrick, she was the greatest tragic actress of her day and excelled as Cordelia, Desdemona, Constance and Otway's Belvidera. That she should also have been a great oratorio singer is a thought that might well leave no more spirit in any modern actress, yet it is as a great contralto that Mrs Cibber is now best remembered, for her singing at the first performance of *Messiah* so moved Handel that he wrote the part of Micah in *Samson* specially for her, perhaps the greatest honour that has ever been accorded to a singer.

It was not that her voice was of exceptionally fine quality; indeed there seems to have been some question as to its merit. Davies tells us that she was not mistress of a voice requisite to a capital singer, and we learn from other sources that it was small though indescribably plaintive; but if it was good enough for Handel, who had at one time or another employed the talents of all the greatest vocalists in Europe, that is all that need concern us, and from that fact a valuable lesson may be learnt by all oratorio singers of the future. It is significant that Handel should have chosen for the performance of his two most sensitive contralto parts a tragic actress, whose voice was not absolutely first-rate, in place of a singer with a magnificent organ but no imagination or musical understanding. No doubt there are to-day many contralto voices finer than Susannah Cibber's, but where is the woman who can convey to her audience the whole awful tragedy of "He was despised" and the heart-shaking pathos of "Return, O God", making us realise that the prophetic inspiration of Isaiah, the dramatic power of Aeschylus and the majesty of Milton's verse are all combined in Handel's music? This Mrs Cibber most certainly did.

When Arne left Eton his father articled him to an attorney for three years, but during this period of

Susannah Maria Cibber

THE ARNE FAMILY

compulsory legal study, he surreptitiously practised music with great assiduity, and contrived to take lessons on the violin from Michael Festing. He made good progress and shortly after the expiry of his articles an incident occurred which determined his future career: his father, calling one day on business at a neighbour's house, found a concert in progress and his son playing among the fiddlers. Some mollification was necessary to restore the composure of the irate father, but, having once realised that music was likely to be a more profitable source of income to his son than law, he allowed him to pursue the art without further restraint, and, as we have already seen, directed his own attention to it as a matter of business.

Arne's first composition of importance was his setting of Addison's *Rosamond*, of which only six songs and a duet still survive. The presentation of this opera was a sort of family party: the principal character was sustained by the composer's sister and the part of the page by his young brother Michael. It was performed at the theatre in Lincoln's Inn Fields in 1733 and proved so successful that it was repeated ten times. At the age of twenty-three Arne had won his spurs and was soon to have regular employment as composer for Drury Lane Theatre.

In 1736 Arne married Cecilia Young, the daughter of the organist of All Hallows Church at Barking. Her father disapproved of the marriage on religious grounds and never forgave his daughter, who soon after became a convert to the Roman Catholic Church.

Mrs Arne was gentle and charming, and the possessor of a soprano voice of unusual compass and flexibility. Burney considered that her style of singing was infinitely superior to that of any other English woman of her time. She gained great distinction in Handel's oratorios, besides singing all the principal parts in the earlier works of her husband, thus contributing in no small measure to his fame. How ill she was repaid by him we shall see in a later chapter, for the time has now come for us to investigate the works that brought fame to Dr Arne, and which, if they were still available for performance, would surely be the delight of modern audiences as they were to those of his own time.

Chapter V

COMUS AND THE JUDGMENT OF PARIS

We have now arrived at what may be considered the golden period of Dr Arne's life, the years during which he produced the three great masques whereon his reputation ought surely to depend, and in which he fully developed the style that was his most natural mode of expression. In later life music of very high quality was to come from him, and not a little of it: the *Judith* choruses are as fine as anything he ever wrote, finer perhaps; and the *Libera Me* has a tender and touching sincerity that we find nowhere else in his work; then, too, we shall see in *The Fairy Prince* a kind of ghostly reflection of the composer's happy, unfaded youth, with all its natural ease, grace and gaiety; but these are instances that occur irregularly, one might almost say accidentally, at a time of life when Arne can no longer be relied upon to be true to himself, or to keep faith with us according to the promise given in his early years.

During these years he poured out music of the rarest loveliness, which might well have been taken as an earnest of still greater things to come. It was his time of triumph. By the three early masques he established his right to be regarded as the greatest

English musician since Purcell, and as such he was proclaimed throughout the land.

The first of these masques was *Comus* which had been adapted from Milton by a certain Dr John Dalton, prebendary of Worcester Cathedral. Dalton introduced into the masque scenes and verses of his own, and characters which knew not Milton, thereby generally transforming an austere Morality play into an elegant and elaborate eighteenth-century pantomime. For this conglomeration of Milton and Dalton, Arne, who was now permanently attached to Drury Lane Theatre, was commissioned to write music. It was performed at the theatre in 1738, and all of us whose palates are not too jaded to drink from the stream of pure melody should be grateful for almost every note of it. It created, as Burney said, an era in English music, and influenced the taste of the whole nation, yet how few out of the thousands of musical enthusiasts who crowd our concert halls year after year could hum the tune of even one of its delicious songs!

The music allotted to Comus and the Pastoral Nymph has spirit, and, where necessary, humour; and there is great tenderness and charm in both the arias sung by the Lady; but it is the Attendant Spirit, the character originally taken by Beard, who is privileged to sing the most beautiful song of all, "Not on beds of fading flow'rs", in which he exhorts his hearers to shun the syren voice of pleasure, and win the height where Virtue sits enthroned. Had Arne himself conscientiously followed this advice,

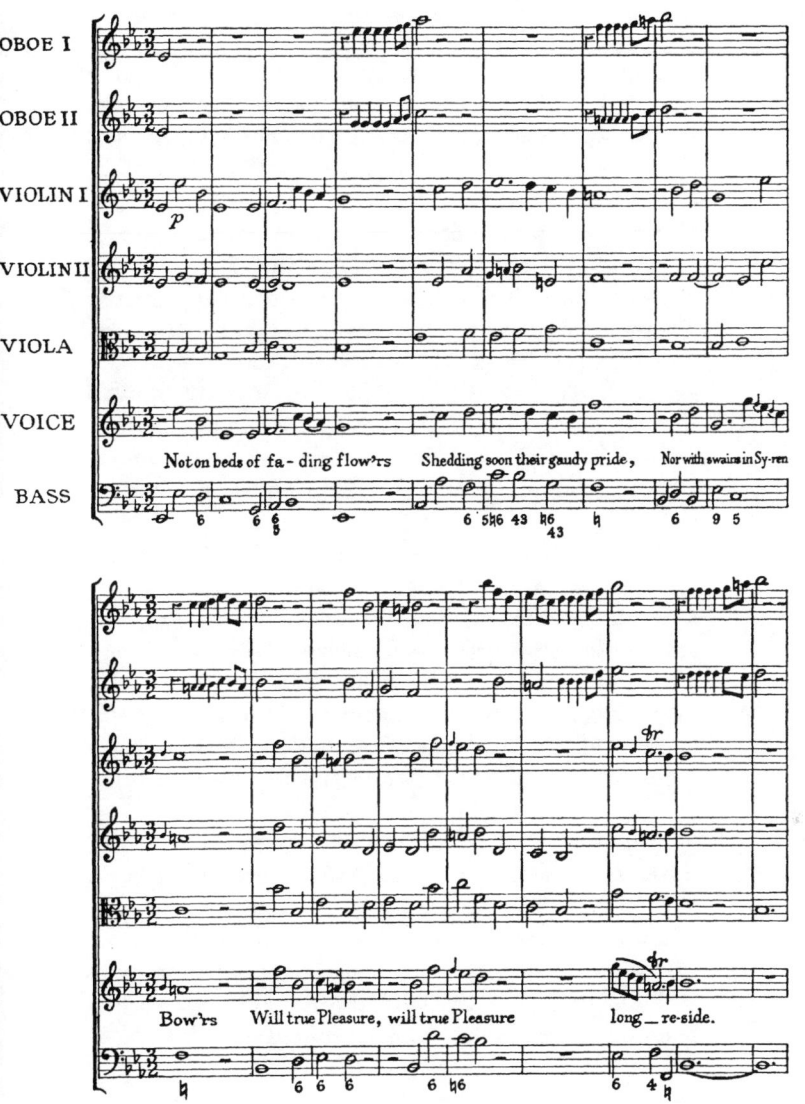

1. From the song "Not on beds of fading flow'rs" (*Comus*).

taking his art more seriously and going on as he had begun, he might have written more of such songs and occupied a throne among the Olympians.

In the music to *Comus*, Arne had found himself, and fixed a standard by which we can judge the whole of the rest of his work; for, although at times it is reminiscent of Handel, yet it has its own very decided individuality and spontaneous expression. There is freshness and natural grace in all the airs, no striving after effect to please the ears of the groundlings, no sacrifice of taste in order to indulge in mere vocal display. It became the model for what was to be recognised for nearly a hundred years as typical English music, and English song deteriorated in proportion as it fell away from this level.

Comus was revived frequently during Arne's life, and the songs in it remained popular for a century after his death. The tenor aria, "Now Phoebus sinketh in the west", is still occasionally sung in the wrong key and by a bass voice, and the elfin setting of "By dimpled brook" has been included in a collection of unison songs for use in schools: one trembles to think of the ponderous treatment it must receive when sung by more than one voice; "How gentle was my Damon's air" has been re-issued under the unpleasing title of "The maiden's lament". The rest of this enchanting music is heard no more.

Two years after *Comus* there followed the second of the masques. This was the setting of Congreve's *The Judgment of Paris*, which forty years earlier had been the subject of a competition between four com-

COMUS, JUDGMENT OF PARIS

posers. This masque contained choruses which were never printed and are nowhere to be found* save for a fragment of the finale which is in manuscript in the British Museum. The songs, duet and trio, with the overture in score were published, and included in the same volume was the "Celebrated Ode in honour of Great Britain".

If we were required to single out for special praise any one entire work of Arne, it would be very hard to reject the claims of *The Judgment of Paris*. The arias have the same melodic beauty as those in *Comus*, but the writing is rather more solid; the composer seems more sure of himself, and to aim at greater things.

The music is appropriate to each character, and attractive as are the arias allotted to Juno and Minerva, it would be impossible to dispute the verdict of Paris given in favour of Venus who wins the golden apple and our highest admiration with a scena of which the beautiful aria, "Nature framed thee sure for loving", puts us in mind of Handel's "Wise men flatt'ring".†

The masque opens with a vision of the three goddesses at whose appearance Paris, the tenor, sings a magnificent aria, "O ravishing delight", wherein he dramatically contrasts his terror of their divine presence with his ecstasy at the sight of their beauty. His fears are allayed by Mercury, another

* It is likely that a great many of Arne's MSS. were destroyed in the fire that burnt Drury Lane Theatre.

† From *Judas Maccabaeus*, composed in 1746.

2. From the overture to *The Judgment of Paris*.

tenor, in one of the most florid arias ever written, "Fear not, mortal", which would tax the powers of any singer, however admirable his breath control; yet there is exquisite grace in these long, flowing, melodious passages, which if sung smoothly and rhythmically need never degenerate into mere meaningless bravura. The result of this effusion of Mercury is that both tenors join together in a cheerful duet.

There is no need to enumerate all the beauties of this enchanting work, but special attention is due to Venus's first aria, "Gentle swain", with a violoncello obbligato and harpsichord accompaniment; also to a trio for the goddesses which, in spite of the constant repetition of rather silly words, contains some very effective part writing, and is one of the principal features of the masque.

It is a thousand pities that the final chorus is lost, for the work as it now stands is unfinished, and in presenting it on the stage the problem must arise of how to bring it to a fitting conclusion. If this doubt were satisfactorily solved, the masque could be performed without any great difficulty, five soloists and a small orchestra being all that would be required. The whole work can be sung in an hour, and with the help of a single classical set and some attractive grouping an entertainment of unusual interest and exceptional charm could be presented to the public by any producer or conductor of sufficient enterprise to attempt something that lies off the beaten track.

Chapter VI

THE MASQUE OF ALFRED AND "RULE, BRITANNIA!"

The year 1740 was an important milestone in Arne's career. On August 1st *The Judgment of Paris* was performed at a fête given by the Prince of Wales at Cliveden, in Buckinghamshire, his beautiful residence on the banks of the Thames, to celebrate the birthday of his daughter, the Princess Augusta, and also the anniversary of the accession of the House of Hanover. For this same fête Arne supplied music to yet another masque, one which was destined to contain his contribution towards the history of England. This was *The Masque of Alfred*, which concludes with the "Ode in honour of Great Britain", now universally known as "Rule, Britannia!".

The text of the masque as performed on this occasion was by the poet Thomson, but it was subsequently altered and lengthened by David Mallet, who incorporated with it Collins's ode, "How sleep the brave", and for this second version Arne wrote more music. The poem treats of the struggles of King Alfred with the Danes and his final victory over them, but the masque is so uninteresting and the characters are so lifeless that no effort should ever be made to revive it on the stage; moreover full justice can be done to the music on the concert plat-

THE MASQUE OF ALFRED

form. The verse on the whole is quite uninspired, but when the king resolves to build a fleet to protect our shores, Thomson rises to the occasion, and poet and musician celebrate England's naval glory by the finest national song in all the world.

But we must not allow "Rule, Britannia!" to distract our attention from the other good things in this masque, for there are many: two soprano songs, "O Peace, thou fairest child of Heaven" and "Sweet valley", the latter accompanied by flute and harpsichord only, are conspicuous; also the brilliant tenor aria, "From the dawn of early morning". There is a stirring march in the best Handelian tradition scored for trumpets and drums in addition to the strings; another joyous soprano aria, "Arise, sweet messenger of morn", and the very attractive "Safe beneath this lowly dwelling" for the same voice. Two more serious songs must be mentioned, one of which, "Guardian angels", became immensely popular, and would still be an enormous help to any singer wishing to sing in church, and whose repertoire of sacred music does not extend much farther than "Angels ever bright and fair" and "My heart ever faithful". The other is a setting of "There honour comes" from Collins's ode. This dirge is one of the most impressive and moving of all Arne's songs, and the effect is enhanced by the wailing notes of its oboe obbligato.

And now for "Rule, Britannia!". The first version of *Alfred* was so short that it was not considered worth while to collect the music for publication, so the "Ode in honour of Great Britain" was published with *The Judgment of Paris*, until Mallet's version of *The Masque of Alfred* appeared in 1745, when it was restored to its original position in the work to which it belonged. From this it is obvious that "Rule, Britannia!" was an immediate success, though by some chance the composer's name was not mentioned in the newspaper report of the first performance. This omission possibly accounts for the fact that at a later date there existed some doubt as to who the composer really was, and by some it was ascribed to Handel. That this error should have been possible is sufficient proof of the music's great merit, yet in the minds of the large majority of people who know it only in its debased form, its musical value is rated no higher than such ebullitions of political hysteria as the "Marseillaise" and "Lilliburlero". Let anyone who is acquainted with Arne's score of this great song imagine that he is listening to the first performance in the gardens of Cliveden, and it should not be difficult for him to recapture something of the enthusiasm that must have animated every member of that privileged audience.

For most of us who are inclined to let our fancies wander back into the past there must be certain "first nights" at which we would fain have been present. What the excitement in the theatre must have been the first time that Portia saved Antonio from the knife of Shylock we can partly guess from what we still feel, even now that every word of that most thrilling of all thrillers is so familiar to us; and

3. Introduction to the song "Rule, Britannia!"
(*The Masque of Alfred*).

what would some of us not give to be transported back to that night at the opera house, when the curtain rose on the first act of *Serse*, the strings gave out the first magical bars of "Ombra mai fu" which Handel had labelled Largo, and Senesino sang the air which still has power, whenever or however it is played, to

> Dissolve us into ecstasies
> And bring all Heav'n before our eyes?

But to return to Cliveden: the *London Daily Post* tells us that there were also "scenes from Mr Rich's Pantomime Entertainment, particularly the Skeleton scene in *Merlin's Cave*, and the Dwarf scene in *Orpheus and Eurydice*; also the famous Le Barberini from Paris performed several dances". A variety show, in fact, with bogies, freaks and a high-kicker to amuse those members of the audience who would be bored with only poetry and music. How little did the Prince of Wales or any of his illustrious guests imagine, as they assembled in those gardens, that before they had dispersed at the close of the evening something would have happened that would make that party for ever memorable in history! Never can "Rule, Britannia!" have sounded more impressive than on that great first night when Lowe, whom Burney declared to be the finest tenor he had ever heard, rolled out the majestic verses, and the chorus burst in with the famous refrain.

And what was the cause of this *succès fou* at Cliveden? To some extent no doubt the patriotic

THE MASQUE OF ALFRED

appeal of the words (which are in truth very fine), and the anniversary that was being celebrated; but above all the inherent dignity of Arne's music. For it is dignity that predominates in "Rule, Britannia!" and it is dignity more than any other quality that has been lost in the process of popularising which followed immediately on the first overwhelming success. Had "Rule, Britannia!" been the jolly Jack Tar sort of song that it has since become, it is doubtful whether it would ever have been heard outside the garden wall of Cliveden, but it is far otherwise. It is infused with dignity, royalty and splendour. Here for instance is the third stanza:

> Still more majestic shalt thou rise,
> More dreadful from each foreign stroke,
> As the loud blast that tears the skies
> Serves but to root thy native oak.

That is grand poetry, and Arne has invested it with a princely garment.

Twice only during the present century has "Rule, Britannia!" been properly performed in a London concert hall. On each occasion the most stirring moments of the Ode were the opening symphony for full orchestra with its exciting drum and trumpet passages and the entry of the chorus at the end of each verse. These moments are unforgettable.*

---

* Another performance was planned to take place towards the end of 1935 at a lecture-concert given for the instruction of London County Council Schools; but the Council authorities vetoed "Rule, Britannia!". They either considered that the

music did not come up to the standard requisite for so august an occasion, or the risk was too great. The very thought of King Alfred's building a navy to protect England from the Danes might put dangerous ideas into the heads of those innocent children who would be seized with an uncontrollable desire to rush to war with Denmark. The performance, therefore, did not take place.

Chapter VII

SHAKESPEARE AND DUBLIN

Before the end of the year 1740 came the first of the series of Shakespeare's comedies for which Arne was commissioned to write new music. This was *As You Like It*, which had not been seen on the London stage for forty years, and its revival excited great interest. *Twelfth Night* followed in 1741; *The Merchant of Venice* in 1742; *The Tempest* and *Love's Labour's Lost* not until 1746 and 1747, but it will be convenient to group these together for our consideration.

Here at least we are on familiar ground. The songs from Shakespeare's plays are the only examples of Arne's work which are still widely known. They do not represent him at his best, and it is of course the poet who in this case has brought fame to the musician, but they are justly admired and deservedly popular. "Where the bee sucks," "Blow, blow, thou winter wind," "Under the greenwood tree," "When daisies pied" are all as fresh to-day as when Arne wrote them. There is a spontaneous gaiety about them which exactly catches the spirit of the words. They refuse to take themselves seriously, and it is this delightful insouciance as well as their irresistible tunefulness that has enabled them to hold their own against all comers. Fresh attempts to set these lyrics are always being made, but so many of these efforts are laboured and inclined to be self-conscious. They may pass muster in the drawing room, but are no good at all for the practical purposes of the stage, and when we think of Ariel, of the Forest of Arden, and of the Merry Dialogue in praise of the Owl and the Cuckoo, it is still with Arne's music that we inevitably associate them in our minds.

In one instance, however, Arne has attempted and indeed achieved something more ambitious. "Come away, Death" is not only intensely pathetic, but exceedingly clever in its harmonies. It belongs to the concert hall rather than to the stage, for it would be almost out of place in such close proximity to Sir Toby Belch and Sir Andrew Aguecheek. Between each of the phrases the tolling bell is heard in the accompaniment, and the tragedy of a broken heart is unfolded in a manner truly piteous.

Before finishing with Shakespeare, it is necessary to refer to the dirge in *Romeo and Juliet*, which quite possibly has not been performed since the production for which it was composed in 1750. It is intended to be sung by the mourners who bear the body of Juliet into the Capulets' tomb. The words are not Shakespeare's, and are not very good, but neither are they so very bad, and here again Arne deals most effectively with the dramatic situation. The dirge is for a three-part chorus accompanied by a flute, strings and a bell. It is quite short; of the three sections of which it is made up the longest has only thirty-two bars. It is of special interest, for, apart from its

SHAKESPEARE AND DUBLIN

intrinsic merit, it is one of the very few specimens of Arne's choral music still in existence, and reveals him in a somewhat unfamiliar mood.

In July 1742 Arne and his wife arrived in Dublin, where they found Handel, who in the previous April had given the first performance of *Messiah* in the Great Room in Fishamble Street, with Mrs Cibber, Arne's sister, in the contralto part. One would have thought that with the presence of Handel and the whole Arne family even the Irish might have been contented, but God was specially good to them this season, and sent David Garrick to entertain them at the theatre.

Was there ever such a collection of genius in one rather small town? We long to know more details. What, for example, did Handel and Garrick make of each other? The great Saxon Bear and the little English actor must have appeared a strangely assorted couple, and may indeed have been so; for though Garrick at a later date became closely concerned with music and musicians, we are told by Charles Dibdin that he was quite unable to distinguish one tune from another; while we know that Handel's knowledge of English was always sketchy (he spoke a kind of Esperanto), and though he could hardly have failed to appreciate Garrick's acting, it is likely that a great deal of Shakespeare was rather lost on him. But this is a digression.

A notice in the *Dublin Journal* of June 1741 describes Arne as the composer of the "Musick of Comus"; it is thereby evident that the masque had already been performed in Dublin and had been well received. This is all the more likely as both Mrs Cibber and Quin, who had respectively played the parts of the Lady and Comus in the original production, had been engaged for the Dublin season, and would almost certainly have introduced Arne's latest success from London.

Music had become one of the distractions of Dublin society owing to the machinations of the Duke of Devonshire, the Lord Lieutenant. It was he who had arranged for Handel's visit, and for the first time the Great Room in Fishamble Street was opened, which was to be for ever memorable as the scene of the first performance of *Messiah* on April 13th, 1742. In this room Handel also gave a series of concerts and, on July 21st of the same year, the arrival of Mr and Mrs Arne was celebrated by a benefit concert which consisted almost entirely of selected works of Arne and Handel sung by Mrs Arne and Mrs Cibber. Handel no doubt was present, and the concert was so successful that it was repeated by request the following week. This was a good start, and Arne left his wife in Dublin at the end of the season, while he went to London with his sister and David Garrick in order to make preparations for a return visit. In a month's time he was back in Dublin, residing with his wife in a house in Aungier Street.

On October 8th Mrs Arne was engaged to sing at the first concert given by the Charitable and Musical Society. The *Dublin Journal* informs us that she sang with universal applause, "though extremely ill of a cold". This is the first intimation we have of her being subject to colds and bad throats which, though trivial in themselves, were, before many years had passed, destined to be the cause of her losing that beautiful quality of voice for which she was so admired.

On December 3rd Mrs Arne sang Handel's "Sweet bird", the flute obbligato being performed on the violin by her husband: this is interesting as showing that Arne must have been a very capable violinist indeed, as anyone familiar with that obbligato will at once recognise. A fortnight later Mrs Arne was again engaged to sing at a concert given "for the benefit and enlargement of Prisoners Confined for Debt". In the following January *Comus* was performed at the Theatre Royal with Arne himself conducting from the harpsichord. For this occasion the orchestra was augmented; Mrs Arne doubled the parts of Sabrina and the Pastoral Nymph, and all the choruses which had been sung in England were included. These are not by Arne, but are mainly selected from Handel's choruses in *L'Allegro* and are not necessary to the performance of the masque. The production was evidently a very special one and required some very elaborate stage management, including the use of wires and trap-doors, for we are told that there were "new habits, machines, risings, sinkings and flyings"; and that it was hoped that it would not be taken ill that no one could be admitted behind the scenes. No doubt a careless intruder might have got involved in the risings and sinkings and perhaps got in the way of the flyings. To meet the extra expense incurred higher prices were charged for admission. The venture succeeded admirably and was repeated four times.

In the spring of 1743 *Alexander's Feast* was performed for charitable purposes; on this occasion Arne conducted and Mrs Arne sang; the chorus consisted of the gentlemen of the choirs of both cathedrals. Three days later Arne had a benefit concert at the Theatre Royal, at which was revived his first opera *Rosamond*. The success of this was so complete that a repetition was announced, but again we find that Mrs Arne had one of her attacks of illness and was forbidden by her doctor to sing. She had sufficiently recovered, however, for the performance to take place a fortnight later.

Arne and his wife remained in Ireland until the autumn of 1744. During this time they scored success after success. *Comus* was in constant demand; *The Judgment of Paris* and *The Masque of Alfred* were played to crowded houses and had to be repeated, and lighter fare was provided in the shape of comic interludes which Arne composed as "a relief from serious performances".

Only one important new work belongs to this period. This is *The Death of Abel*, the first of Arne's two oratorios. We are told so little about it that there is a strong probability that it failed. It was never published and is now lost, all but one song,

SHAKESPEARE AND DUBLIN

the well-known "Hymn of Eve", which except for some rather charming words by Addison is altogether negligible.

Arne's popularity in Dublin was such that nothing was considered to be beyond his powers. We know him as an eminent composer, and we have seen that he was a skilful violinist and conductor; we shall find later that he aspired to be something of a poet, but it might well come as a considerable surprise to us that he should, at least in one instance, have sought to emulate his twice-gifted sister and assumed the role of tragic actor. Yet, sure enough, on January 28th, 1744, he enacted the part of Henry Prince of Wales in the "Second part of *Henry IV*", this "being his first attempt of that kind". It seems also to have been his last, since we never again hear of his acting, but it is always something that he should have been cast for Prince Hal at his first appearance on any stage; and even though he may have played the part badly—as is almost certain to have been the case—it must at least be allowed that he alone of all the famous composers acted professionally in a leading Shakespearean role.

At the close of the season, after two performances of *The Judgment of Paris* and *Alfred* given for their joint benefits, Arne and his wife returned to England. He immediately resumed his connection with Drury Lane Theatre, where he was appointed leader of the orchestra, while Mrs Arne was engaged to sing. He had now reached the zenith of his fame.

A few months after his appointment, an incident

occurred in the theatre in which Arne found himself once again involved in an interesting historical event, though on this occasion he cannot be said to have played a principal part.

It was the year "forty-five". Prince Charles Edward Stuart had been proclaimed king of Scotland and was rapidly marching south with intent to regain England and dispossess the Hanoverian sovereign. There seemed no reason why he should not succeed in his object. The Whig party was in a panic, and the supporters of the foreign dynasty in London were becoming more and more alarmed every day. It was during this period of tension and strain that George II, the little pompous German who had been put on the throne and kept there by the Whig oligarchy as a more or less harmless figurehead who would not interfere with their theories of government, suddenly became an object of popular enthusiasm in the metropolis. On September 28th, at Drury Lane Theatre, the old English tune of "God Save our Noble King", which had already undergone innumerable changes, and was still to experience many more, was sung as an anthem on the stage, was greeted with rapturous applause and encored. The arrangement of the anthem was made by Arne, and the principal singers were Mrs Cibber, Beard and Rheinhold. In order to suit Mrs Cibber's contralto voice it had to be sung in the low key of E flat.

Burney, who at this time was Arne's pupil, made an arrangement of the anthem for Covent Garden

Theatre, where it was equally enthusiastically received, and this display of pious Whiggery was kept up every night on the stage of both theatres until the end of the Jacobite rising. Thus was "God Save the King" established as the Sovereign's official hymn, and thus it became our National Anthem.

Chapter VIII

THE SONGS

Arne had now reached the critical point in his career, and here we may pause for a moment to consider the extent and importance of what he had so far achieved.

By his music to *Comus* he had, as Burney tells us, established an English school of song-writing, influenced the national taste, and guided the genius of all English theatrical composers for the following hundred years. This fact has been entirely overlooked by our latter-day directors of musical fashion, most of whom are eager to pass over all English music between Purcell and Stanford, treating the eighteenth century as a decadent period of Handelian imitations from which they graciously condescend to select a few church anthems as specimens of competent academic workmanship. We might perhaps wonder at this strange indifference towards a period that produced some of our most vigorous choral writing, and many of our best tunes, did we not know that those same arbiters of taste have taken up a patronising attitude even towards Handel himself, and, being utterly incapable of comprehending the vastness of his intellect or realising his infinite subtlety, have sneered at what they only recognise as his robust simplicity, hounding his music from the concert halls, and thinking it no shame that a generation younger than themselves should grow up in complete ignorance of all but one of his oratorios. This being so, it cannot be expected that Handel's contemporaries should have met with any fair measure of appreciation, or received the attention which is their due. It is necessary, therefore, in order that we may form a right estimate of these composers, to supplement our own researches by consulting an older and more trustworthy school of thought than any which prevailed in England during the first quarter of the present century.

We have seen that *Comus* was a very prominent landmark in the history of English music. In this masque and the two that immediately followed it, Arne proved himself an exquisite melodist of the rarest kind; more than that, he could claim to be something of a dramatist and skilled interpreter of words. Moreover, in spite of a certain indebtedness to Handel, he had always remained strongly individual in his songs, and while Handel had absorbed all that was greatest in German and Italian music, was welding the two together and producing a result which we shall ever want words to praise, Arne, without attempting anything on a colossal scale, was warbling his native wood notes, setting an ode in honour of his country grander than any of which other nations could boast, and enriching Shakespeare's lyrics with an imperishable loveliness.

In the year 1745, when Arne was thirty-five, it would not have been unreasonable to hope that he had an even greater destiny to fulfil. As a young man he had won golden opinions; success had come to him quickly and easily; he had been acclaimed in London, in Dublin, and even in Edinburgh which he had not yet visited; but his reputation had now touched the highest point of all its greatness, and just at the moment of life when great things might have been expected of him it was found that he was not the man to perform them. From the first visit to Ireland until his death in 1778 he spent the greater part of his time doing hack-work for the theatre and wasting great natural gifts which might have been far better employed.

This is not to say that all his important work was finished or that his productions of a lighter sort are without interest or merit. Indeed his work for the theatre was of real value, and there resulted from it an agreeable form of entertainment which compares extremely favourably with anything of the kind of a later date; moreover, he succeeded in producing one of the very few English grand operas that has achieved a furore and held the stage for three-quarters of a century. Flashes of genius of a higher sort were still to burst forth at intervals, and at least three works of outstanding merit belong to the later years, but this is not enough to fulfil the promise of the early masques and we are disappointed that the composer of *The Judgment of Paris* left the highest peaks of music, except on a single occasion—the *Judith* choruses—unscaled.

The truth is that Arne's reputation soon after this date began to decline in every direction. To the end of his life he remained eminent as a teacher of singing, and his songs written for Vauxhall and Ranelagh Gardens had a wide and popular appeal; *Artaxerxes* increased his fame with a public that paid more attention to the mellifluous warbling of Charlotte Brent than to the music which she sang; but musicians such as Burney began to have their doubts, and Hawkins, though out of personal spite, completely omits Arne's name from his *History of Music*.

Arne was not a man of strong character, and it would seem that success, as is too often the case in the world of the theatre, did not improve him. Fanny Burney, writing long after his death and that of her father, has left us the following unprepossessing description of him:

"Thoughtless, dissipated, and careless, he neglected or rather scoffed at all other but musical reputation. And he was so little scrupulous in his ideas of propriety, that he took pride, rather than shame in being publicly classed, even in the decline of life, as a man of pleasure. Such a character was ill qualified to form or protect the morals of a youthful pupil, and it is probable that not a notion of duty ever occurred to Dr Arne, so happy was his self-complacency in the fertility of his invention and the ease of his compositions, and so dazzled by the brilliancy of his success in his powers of melody—which, in truth, for the English stage, were in sweetness and variety unrivalled—that, satisfied and flattered by the practical exertions and the popularity of his fancy, he had no ambition, or rather, no thought concerning the theory of his art."

Good Mme D'Arblay has in the above passage tended to confuse private morality with artistic conscience, but we see what she means, and the information was doubtless given to her by her father, who had the best of reasons for knowing what he was talking about. Arne in fact was a waster and a roué, parts which he had no doubt inherited. Having attained a great reputation he was content to rest on his laurels and to go on supplying light music for a not too fastidious public, thereby keeping himself employed and earning a sufficient income which he squandered away.

Besides his permanent engagement at Drury Lane Theatre, Arne was now appointed composer to Vauxhall, Mary-le-bone, and Ranelagh Gardens. This marked another very definite stage in his career, and before examining the quality of the music that he produced for these places of public entertainment it may be as well to consider briefly what the functions of these gardens were.

The pages of *Evelina* and other novels of the period have made us familiar with certain aspects of the Spring Gardens at Vauxhall, and what we know about them is no doubt applicable to the other haunts of the same nature. To these gardens the fashionable world of London resorted in the summer evenings to amuse itself in whatever way it liked, and not only the world of fashion, for a good sprinkling of the underworld went along too. There were arbours where parties met for supper, side-shows and entertainments of every description, laid out gardens and lawns, cascades and grottoes lighted by lanterns, long vistas to delight the eye, and firework displays, all arranged with the elegance and grace that characterised the epoch of which they were the special attribute.

These gardens were the peculiar creation of the eighteenth century; they overlapped into the nineteenth, but their glory had by then departed, and having become merely haunts of ill-repute were brought to an end, Vauxhall surviving the others by several decades.

From the novelists and writers of memoirs we can form a fairly accurate picture of Vauxhall with its many scenic attractions, its splendidly dressed aristocracy, its ludicrously overdressed cits and their wives, and the inevitable representatives of the oldest profession in the world, who in spite of the salutary and awful warnings of Hogarth must have found excellent hunting there. But in the midst of all this glitter and glamour, is it fully realised that there was always music to be heard by those who cared to hear it, and that that music was Handel's? It is a staggering thought. Such a thing would at the present day be impossible. Indeed soon after the dawn of the nineteenth century with the growth of democracy and its handmaid, vulgarity, classical music played in the open air before a promiscuous audience would have been altogether unthinkable. We cannot easily imagine the bandstands in Hyde Park filled by orchestras which would daily perform Handel's Concerti Grossi and the Brandenburg

Concertos. The experiment, given time, would probably be successful, but what Commissioner of Works would have the audacity to make it? It has been well said by one of the finest and most cultured of our living actors that "the English people are the most musical in Europe, but the music must be bad". In the reign of George II this was not so: although under the administration of Walpole and his Whigs the germ of democracy was beginning to spread through the nation like a cancerous growth, yet the upper class had not yet thought it necessary to conform to the standards of taste and behaviour that marked the lower grades of the community, but still retained a degree of culture and refinement that waned in the course of the next century, and which is at the present time altogether insufficient to distinguish it from the classes to which it has so generously surrendered every other privilege.

It would be, of course, ridiculous to pretend that the entire *beau monde* of the eighteenth century was capable of appreciating Handel's music, or that the majority of them would not have preferred the native ballads which Arne dealt out so lavishly to them. Had it been so there would have been no *Beggar's Opera* and Handel would not have been bankrupt twice and driven into exile. But among the patrons of Vauxhall there must have been a very large proportion who had a cultured taste for music; for an organ and orchestra, exposed on one side to the open air, were erected, on which Handel played his concertos, and among the most prominent orna-

THE SONGS

ments of the gardens was the statue of Handel, the first work executed by Roubiliac in England.* Handel was clearly a name to conjure with, for Tyers, the lessee of the Spring Gardens, arranged for the rehearsal of the Firework Music to take place at Vauxhall prior to its performance in the Green Park. Twelve thousand people listened to this rehearsal and the traffic became so congested that the passage over London Bridge was stopped for three hours. Did Handel among other things perhaps beget the London traffic problem?

At Ranelagh we hear of choruses from the oratorios and a performance of *L'Allegro*, while Festing led the orchestra and Beard sang. A description of Ranelagh on the occasion of a jubilee masquerade in honour of the Peace of Aix-la-Chapelle is given by Horace Walpole, who concludes by saying that it pleased him more than anything he ever saw. Walpole fancied himself a judge of such matters, and would not have been too easy to please, so we may assume that the masquerade was satisfactory from an aesthetic point of view.

It is sad to look upon Vauxhall, now one of the most sordid and dirtiest districts of London, and to think of its past glory; but Ranelagh has had a happier fate. On the east side of the gardens of Chelsea Hospital, railed off from the rest of the grounds, there still remains about an acre of flower garden beautifully kept, and carefully guarded. Here

* This statue is still to be seen at the top of the staircase of Novello and Co's premises in Wardour Street.

dogs are not allowed to enter, no, not even on the lead, and their owners can only survey this Promised Land from the Pisgah of the flowerless field that adjoins it, or through the railings that divide it from the Chelsea Embankment. Near to this enclosure two hundred years ago stood the great rotunda in which Handel conducted his oratorios, and for which Arne wrote innumerable songs; and here at the age of eight Mozart played his own compositions on the organ and the harpsichord.

Such then were the Public Gardens to which Arne was appointed composer, and such were the audiences he had to entertain. For his singers he had the best that London could provide: his own wife, Lowe and Rheinhold, and a few years later his son Michael, then a little boy of ten. Arne held this position until the end of his life, turning out songs, duets and comic dialogues, which were eventually collected and published under such names as *The Agreeable Musical Choice*, *Lyric Harmony*, *The Vocal Grove*, etc.

Burney insists that by these songs the musical taste of the nation was raised and an English school of song-writing founded; this however had already been done by *Comus*, and the bulk of songs composed for the gardens falls very far short of that standard. But if we find that the greater number of these songs are of no very high quality, we must take into consideration the fact that they were written for the general, not for the musical, public. Simplicity, melody and humour were what was aimed at;

nothing that could make any great demands on the understanding, or the deeper emotions. For this purpose Arne chiefly made use of the ballad style and verse form with which English audiences are so familiar, and very often the lately imported Scottish rhythms make their appearance too. The harmonies are simple and unadventurous, and though no doubt an orchestra was originally employed, in most cases a harpsichord is the only accompaniment needed. The words, which as often as not Arne wrote himself, are of the Colin and Phyllis variety and usually devoid of any kind of merit; sometimes a little humour is attempted, but seldom with much success.

Wading through the innumerable collections of these songs we are struck by the fluent and graceful melodies, and very occasionally by a genuine inspiration, but on the whole the search becomes monotonous and wearisome, even though a real gem like "Lotharia" will sometimes be found. This beautiful little song occurs again in *Love in a Village* set to different words. It has been republished. "When forced from dear Hebe to go", with words altered from Shenstone, stands well above the average, having both charm and humour, and "Polly Willis" is still a favourite.

There is, however, another side to all this. Though Arne's reputation in the judgment of posterity may not have benefited by the Vauxhall songs, they were largely responsible for his popularity with his contemporaries, and by his position as Director of

Music to the Public Gardens a singularly happy compromise was effected. For, whereas a greater or less adaptable composer would have written over the heads of his audience, and a lesser man would have written down to its level, Arne met the English public halfway, and, thoroughly understanding it, produced the sort of music that was wanted, without ever falling below a certain standard of excellence, thus keeping the national taste for melody at a higher level than it was ever again to reach.

With the help of such accomplished artists as Mrs Arne and Kitty Clive even some of the less attractive songs would still have power to charm us, and we may well look back with envy to a generation whose light music and popular ballads were provided by Dr Arne, who, though sometimes swayed by foreign influences, remained essentially English and was, in the words of John Hullah, "the most thoroughly national of all our song writers".

Chapter IX

MRS ARNE

The important event of the year 1746 was the revival at Drury Lane Theatre of *The Tempest* in which "Where the bee sucks" was heard for the first time, sung by Kitty Clive as Ariel. *Love's Labour's Lost* followed the year after: *Much Ado About Nothing* in 1749; and *Romeo and Juliet* with its dirge in 1750.

Meanwhile Mrs Arne had gone to Dublin with her sister Mrs Lampe, who was also a singer. Here she suffered again from frequent attacks of illness, which prevented her from singing during the early part of the season, but she recovered and took part in a number of Handel's oratorios including *Esther*, *Solomon* and *Acis and Galatea*. She is next heard of singing at Covent Garden in the revival of *Harlequin Sorcerer*, an old pantomime for which Arne wrote new music. It contains a very attractive duet, "Damon and Florella".

In 1754 Arne visited Edinburgh where a concert of vocal and instrumental music was given for his benefit, and in 1755 he and his wife were back again in Dublin for the third time. On this occasion they were accompanied by Arne's most illustrious pupil, Charlotte Brent, who was soon to have the whole of London at her feet, and who from all accounts must have been one of the finest sopranos that this country ever produced.

Arne was eminent as a teacher of singing, and it is to his credit that here at least he took endless trouble, insisting on clear articulation, and inspiring enthusiasm in his pupils. He also possessed the rare faculty, one which he shared with Handel, of keeping his singers in subjection, and snubbing their conceit. He did not always express his opinion in the kindest possible way, and a story is told of how he once judged between two male singers who were competing for a prize. Having listened to both, he said to the one who had sung second, "You, sir, are the worst singer I have ever heard." "Then I have won the prize," exclaimed the first. "Oh, no!" said Arne, "You are not a singer at all."

During the Dublin season the new opera *Eliza* was brought out, after a postponement caused by one of Mrs Arne's usual attacks of illness. We see these becoming gradually more frequent, and when at last she was well enough to sing, the *Dublin Journal*, in its account of the performance, mentions that she had the misfortune of a violent hoarseness, and rose from her bed in a fever in order to perform.

Eliza, to which we shall refer again later, was very well received, and twice repeated. There were also performances of *Rosamond* and *The Tempest*, Charlotte Brent appearing as Ariel. The ever-popular *Comus* was revived on two occasions and a third time for the composer's benefit. At the end of the season for the joint benefit of Mr and Mrs Arne *The*

Masque of Alfred was sung in the manner of an oratorio.

Arne left Dublin never to return. He also left his wife to whom he was to return only after twenty years. Not for long had he been faithful to the charming and excellent woman who had to so large a degree contributed to his success, and though we are not actually told so, it seems highly probable that Mrs Arne's frequent illnesses were to some extent attributable to her husband's unkindness. His son, Michael, who had been born as far back as 1740, was said by many authorities, of whom Burney was one, to have been illegitimate.

Michael Arne was to become almost as prolific a song-writer as his father, and it is the strange irony of Dr Arne's fate that, whereas almost all his fine work is now forgotten, he should still be remembered for something that he never did at all. He did *not* write "The lass with a delicate air". That was one of Michael's songs, and he is welcome to it, yet week after week it appears on concert programmes as being by "Arne", which of course implies Thomas Augustine.

Mrs Arne remained in Dublin broken in health and spirits, and very poor. She gave a concert with her niece, Polly Young, in the April of 1757, but immediately after retired from public life. There is a most distressing account of her given about this time in a letter of Mrs Delaney who describes her as an object of compassion, humbled, half-starved, with the bloom gone from her voice and from her face. Mrs Delaney had met her in the house of a Mr Bayley who, pitying her distress, had arranged for her to give Miss Bayley singing lessons. The letter goes on: "She has been severely used by a bad husband, and suffered to starve, if she had not met with charitable people."

In January 1759 Mrs Arne returned to the concert platform and sang at a concert given for her benefit. This was the last occasion on which she appeared before the Dublin public, but her loss of voice can only have been temporary, as we hear of her many years later, in 1768 at the age of fifty-seven, singing the part of Mandane in *Artaxerxes*, an extraordinary feat at that age, and one which, as we shall see in discussing the opera, could only have been attempted by a vocalist of the most exceptional technical ability.

At this point of the story and before dealing any further with Arne's musical productions, it will not be inappropriate to pursue to its conclusions the course of his relations with his wife. It is not an edifying tale, nor is there anything particularly uncommon about it, but it serves to show the instability of his character, and explains, though perhaps indirectly, how a man of so mean a spirit proved incapable of maintaining a high standard of excellence in his work.

We know that in 1756 Arne left his wife, and soon afterwards we hear of her being in great distress and want. There does not seem to have been the smallest excuse for this. He was permanently engaged to compose music for the two great London theatres as well as for the Public Gardens, and he must have been drawing a sufficient salary to have been able to keep his wife at least from penury; yet in 1770 she sends him a lawyer's letter threatening him with legal proceedings, and complaining that the allowance he had been making her "fell greatly short of supplying her with common necessaries, and that even that small sum was in arrear". Arne's reply is contemptible and cowardly. He expresses surprise at the tone of his wife's letter, and assumes an air of injured innocence, declaring that he has had no employment for some months, and has been robbed by a servant, and consequently involved in debts, but that he has given her money whenever he has had it to give. He threatens in his turn that he will give her nothing if she should "drive him to resentment, when he is willing to act conformable to the laws of religion, peace and love". He also adopts the most cowardly expedient of trying to throw blame upon his wife, accusing her of ungenerous treatment of himself and imprudent management of her affairs. It is a letter full of cant and self-pity, that betrays a meanness of spirit which would deceive nobody. Mrs Arne's gentle answer was sent through an attorney. "Mrs Arne wishes it was in her power to avoid calling on him for a subsistence. Her loss of Dr Arne's affections has been a misfortune she has laboured under too many years, and without doing him the least injury, she has behaved with that affection and justice that will give her satisfaction in her last moments. She hopes Dr Arne has not so little humanity as to add to her misery by refusing her a necessary subsistence sufficient to provide her with common necessaries." She concludes pathetically enough by saying that if that is paid her she must content herself with wearing out an unhappy life deprived of the comfort which she had a right to expect from her husband. There can be no doubt as to the sincerity of this appeal, and that the letter is written by a much-wronged woman still devoted to her husband.

We do not hear of any mistress or any special attachment that diverted Arne's affections from his wife. Not even that excuse can be urged as a slight palliation for his unkindness, and one is simply left to conclude that he was wasting his time in aimless philandering and pointless extravagance.

It is abundantly clear that he was also losing the respect of his fellow-artists and associates. The young composer with brilliant gifts had turned into an elderly roué, doing second-class work. We have heard Dr Burney's verdict on his character, and there now began a course of bickering with David Garrick about various matters connected with the theatre and the choice of singers. By their letters, we see, as time goes on, the breach between the two becoming wider and relations more strained. The tone of their correspondence grows less friendly and more formal. Arne is full of grievances, hurt in his feelings and wounded in his pride, complaining that Garrick holds both him and his judgment in slight estimation. Garrick's replies are frigidly civil, and snubbing in tone. We get the impression that the actor was treating the musician in a high-handed and rather ungenerous fashion, and that the latter had some grounds for complaint, but by this time Garrick had probably found out exactly what Arne was worth and was holding him in lofty disdain.

Two letters that Arne wrote to Garrick on the subject of *King Arthur* are interesting as throwing light on his estimate of one of Purcell's most important works, and on his idea that he could himself improve upon it by bringing it up to date.

The long scene of the sacrifice in Act I may have a solemn and noble effect, provided that the last air and chorus be performed as I have now composed it; the introductory air to be sung by Champness, which, being highly spirited, will carry off with an éclat an otherwise dull, tedious, antiquated suite of chorus; besides which that song, as set by Purcell, is very indifferent, and no way proper for a woman, where a troop of warriors are assembled, to bribe their idols for a success in battle.

The following song and chorus "Come if you dare" is tolerable, but so very short of that intrepidity and spirited defiance pointed at by Dryden's words and sentiments, that I think you will only have to hear what I have composed to make you immediately reject the other. The air "Let not a moon-born elf" is after the first two bars of Purcell, very bad. Hear mine. All the other solo songs of Purcell are infamously bad; so very bad that they are the objects of sneer and ridicule to the musicians. I wish you would allow me to doctor this performance. I would certainly make it pleasing to the public.

Garrick only partially acceded to these arrogant proposals and the production of *King Arthur* in 1770 thus became a hotch-potch of the two styles. Arne was exceedingly proud of his additional music and perhaps rightly so: he says that for air and mastership he had never excelled the principal songs. Purcell's music seemed to him more suited to the cathedral than to the theatre, and not to the taste of a modern audience. We know this last phrase well, and are sick of hearing it. It is the excuse that is always given for the mangling of old masterpieces by injudicious editors and ignorant producers, who, because they are utterly deficient in taste themselves, wish us to believe that the modern public must necessarily be so too.

Arne has been reviled for this heresy, but he was only committing the error of judgment common to every age. Purcell's style was to him old-fashioned. Weelkes he could appreciate, and he said of the madrigal, "The Nightingale", that "the mastership and genius of this production may serve as a specimen of the state of music at that time, 1608". That period was farther away from him, and he could view it in true perspective, but Handel and the luxuriant Italian melodies must have made the music of Purcell and his contemporaries sound strangely archaic to many eighteenth-century ears.

The process of "bringing up-to-date" is sometimes commercially profitable, but very rarely desirable. It is doubtful, however, whether the possibilities of that particular art were fully developed until recently when the London public was bidden to a bewildering production of something advertised as Mendelssohn's *Elijah*, wherein among other surprises, in the place of the overture, a ballet was danced to music from the *Walpurgisnacht*, and "O rest in the Lord" was sung with a superimposed descant of soprano voices!

We have dwelt so long on Arne's misdemeanours and his wife's distresses that it is consoling to find that the story has something of a happy ending. In 1777, after a separation of more than twenty years, the pair were reunited through the accidental agency of their great-niece, a little girl of ten.

The child's mother, Mary Barthelemon, whom we already know as Polly Young, used to visit her uncle to receive from him her aunt's separate maintenance money, and on one occasion her daughter accompanied her. The mother declared, on leaving, that she was tired of coming continually for the same purpose and suggested that Arne should be reconciled to his wife, with whom he could have no fault to find. Arne flew into a passion and became violent, whereupon the child, who was sitting on his knee, burst into tears. The old man, who was very fond of her, was so affected that a few days later he wrote to say that "if his dear old wife would be reconciled he would be happy to see her, and her nephew and niece with their dear child, at dinner on Sunday". The reconciliation was so easily effected that one can only wish that the idea had been put into his head before, and that so many years of happiness had not been lost to them both, through what was in all probability mere selfishness and obstinacy. They lived very happily together for a few months, but before a year had passed Dr Arne was dead.

A contemporary writer records that "notwithstanding the number and excellence of his publications, Dr Arne left little or no property behind him; a circumstance which will not appear extraordinary to those who consider his real character and life. He was naturally fond of vicious pleasure, to which he sacrificed every other consideration." This is a severe indictment, and though perhaps no exaggeration, it will be more charitable to remember the closing scene of his life, the last months spent in perfect happiness with his wife, the memory of which must have been a great comfort to her during the remainder of her life. What little he had to leave Arne left to her and to his son Michael, and these two were also to benefit by any profit produced by the performance or publication of his music.

Mrs Arne survived her husband by eleven years, dying in October 1789 at the age of seventy-nine. She was buried in the vaults of St Martin's-in-the-Fields. To the end of her life she remained a strict and pious Catholic, "observing all the fast days with a rigour suitable to the austerity of primitive times, although the Church's discipline excused such habits of severe self-denial in its members at her time of life". A few days after her death Dr Burney wrote a letter to her niece, Mrs Barthelemon, of which the following is an extract:

I profited more in my studies by the advantage of accompanying her in her vocal exercises than by any instructions which the Doctor had leisure to give me. She was indeed not only desirous of my professional improvement, but had a parental attention to my morals and conduct. As long as I remained under the same roof, I tried everything in my power, and not unsuccessfully, to contribute to domestic harmony; and I flatter myself if I had continued longer with them, the union would have been of longer duration.

The Doctor, rest his soul! with all his genius and abilities was too *volage* at every period of his life to merit the title of a good family man, and soon after I quitted him, I heard with grief that our late dear worthy friend was no longer under the same roof. I lost sight of her, but never forgot the goodness of her heart, or the talents and professional merit of her younger years. There was a time when her voice, shape and manner of singing were superior to those of any female singer in the country.

Chapter X

OPERAS AND BALLAD OPERAS

The University of Oxford conferred the degree of Doctor of Music upon Arne in July 1759: for this he composed an ode which is now lost. He was originally self-taught and is sometimes said to have been poorly versed in the science of music, yet in the instrumental works he shows himself a complete master of counterpoint, more particularly in the fugue of the overture to *The Judgment of Paris* in which the subject and its counterpoints are inverted and treated with learning and skill, and yet with great freedom and simplicity of effect. Previously to taking his degree he had been studying under Pepusch, but at a much earlier date he produced many examples of fine contrapuntal writing.

Any attempt to arrange the various styles of Arne's music in periods is doomed to failure. There is no definite time at which he can be said to have changed from one style to another. Dr Burney cites the year 1762 as the date at which he abandoned his natural mode of expression for the fripperies of Italian opera, thereby suggesting that it was not until he wrote *Artaxerxes* that Arne adopted this new manner. But though *Artaxerxes* was undoubtedly the culminating point of this development, yet for many years before that Arne had

OPERAS AND BALLAD OPERAS 65

shown a gradual tendency to elaborate his airs with unnecessary ornamentation, and to abandon the pure classical style of his masques for something more artificial. The oratorio *Judith* which precedes *Artaxerxes* by one year is not wholly free from these extravagancies; the opera *Eliza*, considerably earlier still, is permeated with them; while even the 1745 version of *The Masque of Alfred* is slightly tainted.

There is a strong probability that from the time when Arne took up his duties at Drury Lane Theatre in 1745 he had to find a style suited to the taste of the theatre public, and he made it his business to give them what they wanted. He gradually found out what the opera public wanted too and gave them *Artaxerxes*, which, with *Comus*, proved the most successful of all his works and held the stage right into the nineteenth century.

But it would be incorrect to assert that Arne had for ever relinquished the style of the masques, the style which we now recognise as the Handelian idiom (though in reality it prevailed throughout all the music of the first half of the eighteenth century), for it reaches its climax in the *Judith* choruses, and recurs again with a difference in *The Fairy Prince* as late as 1771.

The truth of the matter lies perhaps in the fact that Arne was very greatly influenced by the merits or demerits of his libretti, perhaps to a greater degree than he himself was aware; for it is remarkable that in almost every case where the words are good his music is correspondingly interesting, whereas his settings of trumpery ballads and of his own very indifferent translations of Metastasio are for the most part quite unconvincing. It is therefore evident that his style varied not so much according to period as in accordance with the quality and genre of his libretto.

Now most of the middle period of Arne's life was spent in composing music for ballad operas and farces, and it is evidently this class of work that provoked the scorn of Dr Burney and outraged the audience who found specimens of it in the Italian opera, *Olimpiade*. Burney was right, for though there are some charming things and much good funning to be found among these comedies, yet Arne, in devoting so much time to them, deliberately lowered his standard and frittered away a genius that should have been employed to better purpose.

Nevertheless wholesale condemnation of these ballad operas would be most unwise. There are always exceptions, and the best of these would provide an evening's entertainment aesthetically equal to such *opere buffe* as Pergolesi's *La Serva Padrona* or Méhul's *Le Jeune Sage et le Vieux Fou*, and just as diverting as the operas of Gilbert and Sullivan.

There is good music in *May-Day or the Little Gipsy*, and at least one light opera, popular in its own time, has attracted a great deal of attention in recent years. This is *Thomas and Sally, or the Sailor's Return* which was produced at Covent

OPERAS AND BALLAD OPERAS 67

Garden in 1760 with Beard and Charlotte Brent in the cast.

It is just a little exasperating to the student of Arne that, when all his best and most important works are so sadly neglected, a trifle like *Thomas and Sally* should have been picked out for revival at least four times in the course of the last ten years. There is nothing in the music to justify this re-awakening of interest, when compared with any one of the masques; nor does it add one inch to Arne's stature as a composer. Wherein, then, lies the merit of this little farce which still seems to have so much life in it?

One great recommendation is that it has only four characters, two sopranos and two tenors, and a small male chorus. It is also quite short and fits conveniently into a double or triple bill. These advantages account very largely for its popularity, but the real secret of its charm lies in its excellent libretto. The play is by Isaac Bickerstaffe, who was an exceedingly competent writer of comedies. His plots have invention, and his dialogue wit that we look for in vain from any other English playwright between Farquhar and Sheridan, and Arne, wretched poet though he was himself, had a fine taste for literature serious or comic, and, as we have already seen, seldom failed to take full advantage of the opportunities afforded.

The plot of *Thomas and Sally* is an amusing burlesque of the time-honoured story of the simple village maiden, who during her sailor lover's absence at sea is subjected to the dishonourable attentions of the wealthy squire. The squire is assisted in his schemes by a matron who, never having had any character to lose, finds Sally's notions of chastity somewhat irksome. The sailor boy arrives home just in time to rescue Sally from the squire's aggressions, and the two lovers are joined in happy wedlock.

It all sounds very simple and ingenuous, but actually there is a great deal more in it than that, for in the hands of Isaac Bickerstaffe the characters and sentiments they express are delightfully exaggerated; Sally's virtue and Thomas's nautical and patriotic fervour are most amusingly overdrawn; and the words of the recitatives are ridiculous enough, which if sung in the proper spirit can produce a most ludicrous effect.

Bickerstaffe has written well, and Arne has done exactly what is required of him. With the unerring sense of the stage that never fails him, he has given point to all the little jokes, and exactly suited his music to the dramatic situation. The result is very disarming and we are forced into the admission that *Thomas and Sally* is first-class entertainment of its kind. Sally's aria, "Grant me, ye powers", has a melting strain foreshadowing the arias of Mozart's woe-begone ladies; the love-duet at the end is very appealing indeed; and the scene where Thomas delivers Sally from the squire has effective writing for all three characters. In the duet for Sally and the squire, where he presses his suit, very effective use is made of an unusual rhythm: each character sings a verse in three-two time, which changes into three-four for the concerted section. Their second duet, "Well met, pretty maid", in which they sing alternate verses, goes with a swing that might put the most carping critic into a good temper.

Thomas and Sally was a novelty in 1760. It was a real opera with the action carried on in recitative in the place of spoken dialogue. Since Purcell's *Dido and Aeneas* there had only been one attempt at grand opera in English; this was Galliard's *Calypso and Telemachus* produced in 1712. It failed, though it is said to contain a number of beautiful things, and the field was left clear for Italian opera, mirth-provoking though it was and always will be to the average Englishman, whose common-sense or sense of humour can only tolerate opera in comic form.

There was another innovation in *Thomas and Sally*: the clarinet, which in this work made its appearance for the first time in England and almost for the first time in Europe.

The best of all the ballad operas is *Love in a Village*. The play is again by Bickerstaffe, and for it Arne collected and adapted well-known tunes by other composers and wrote some original music of his own. All the best songs are by him; so also is the lovely little duet, "All I wish", and the sparkling trio, "Well, come, let us hear what the swain must possess", in which the semiquavers of the accompanying bass instruments add a delightful vitality to the graceful lilt of the voice parts. And can there be many better comic songs than Lucinda's warning to her maiden aunt? The words are worth quoting:

> Believe me, dear aunt,
> If you rave thus and rant,
> You'll never a lover persuade;
> The men will all fly
> And leave you to die
> (Oh! terrible chance) an old maid.
>
> How happy the lass,
> Must she come to the pass,
> Who ancient virginity 'scapes;
> 'Twere better on earth
> Have five brats at a birth
> Than in hell be a leader of apes.

These words give Arne a great opportunity, and he makes full use of it.

Eliza, which is styled an opera, is more properly a ballad opera, for though the arias are on the whole longer and more pretentious than is the rule in these lighter productions, yet to judge by the music it is not intended to be taken too seriously. It is Arne's tribute to Gloriana which he pays in the usual coin. There is the customary quota of happy nymphs and swains; there are the bold yeomen who transform their pruning hooks into swords for the sake of old England, and beat them back again into pruning hooks when the danger is over, and Art and Religion once more flourish unmolested under the vigilant eye of the Queen. An eighteenth-century "Merry England" in truth, wherein Britannia shakes her lance with a vocal roulade on almost every page, and the Spaniard is hated with a right good will!*

The music of this rather blatant display of patriotism is compounded of the ballad and the flamboyant styles, both of which serve their purpose admirably. Only one song, the first in the opera, is of very high quality, but several of the smaller ones are distinctly pleasing, and in the hands of really first-rate singers even the lance-shaking might be made to sound quite effective.

In 1762, two years after *Thomas and Sally*, Arne, this time in good earnest, hurled his bold challenge at Italian opera, confident that the English language could be made as tractable as Italian, and that English opera could be established in London. He translated Metastasio's *Artaxerxes* himself, and presented it at Covent Garden with a powerful cast, which included Charlotte Brent, Beard, and the famous Italian *castrati*, Tenducci and Perelli. His triumph was complete, and though the language and the music were totally unsuited to each other, and the cause of English opera made no permanent headway, *Artaxerxes* enjoys the distinction of being one of the few English operas to achieve fame. It remained in constant demand for three-quarters of a century and was still being sung as late as 1838.

This was indeed a full-blown grand opera with recitatives and a turgid plot. The climax of the flamboyant style was reached, and Arne employed

* *Eliza* would certainly be vetoed by the London County Council. (See page 32 in Chap. VI.)

every device known to composers for winning popular applause. The arias were encrusted with ornament, and the part of Mandane, specially written to display the exceptional ability of Charlotte Brent, was for years to come regarded as the supreme test of a coloratura soprano's technique.

The success of this opera was altogether out of proportion to its merits, and it was condemned by Burney and other discriminating judges as meretricious and artificial. There was always a section of the public which, even in Handel's day, preferred the simple English melodies to the elaborate methods of Italian opera and objected to the introduction of Italian singers on to the English stage. The hostility of this section was again aroused by the extravagant embellishments of the arias in *Artaxerxes* and the engagement of the two Italian singers, Tenducci and Perelli. Arne and his Italians were bespattered by Churchill's venom in *The Rosciad* where we read the following lines:

> Let Tommy Arne with usual pomp of style
> Whose chief, whose only merit's to compile
> * * * * *
> Publish proposals, laws for taste prescribe,
> And chant the praise of an Italian tribe;
> Let him reverse kind Nature's first decrees,
> And teach e'en Brent a method not to please:
> But never shall a truly British age
> Bear a vile race of eunuchs on the stage:
> The boasted work's called National in vain,
> If one Italian voice pollute the strain.

Churchill, the most bitter of all English satirical poets, was a good hater, and it is more than probable that he disliked Arne personally or he would not so ungenerously have singled out the least inspired of all his important compositions, and ignored his really fine work; but it must be admitted that in so far as this passage is an attack on *Artaxerxes* it is fully justified. Scarcely an aria in the whole opera sincerely expresses any emotion at all, or is the outcome of any genuine feeling. There is the usual flow of ingratiating melody which we never seek in vain from Arne, but it is almost everywhere disfigured by vocal gymnastics whose chief aim is to excite wonder at the skill of the gymnast. It is perhaps for this reason that one of the only unpretentious airs became and remained until recent years a great favourite among all the songs that Arne ever wrote. This is "Water parted from the sea", a simple, straightforward melody of no special beauty, which ends with the composer's stalest and tritest "tag", but which comes as a welcome contrast in the midst of so much ranting.

Yet when all this has been objected to *Artaxerxes*, it is still the work of an accomplished musician. There is a solidity and sureness of touch in the handling of even the coloratura arias; their rhythms are strong and they have nothing in common with the emasculate quaverings of later Italian opera as exemplified by Donizetti and Bellini. Freer use is made of orchestral colour than in Arne's earlier works, and the accompaniments of the arias are quite frequently independent of the vocal line.

In music, as in drama, what is displeasing in the study may be very effective in performance, and if *Artaxerxes* were revived to-day by way of experiment in a reasonably small theatre and with a prima donna whose skill came within measurable distance of Charlotte Brent's, it is not impossible that it might once more prove at least a nine days' wonder. But it would require to be retranslated into Italian. Arne did himself a great disservice by his English libretto. It is extremely bad, and even were it a great deal better, it would be totally unsuited to the music. The English language is much too heavy artillery for these elegant unrealities, and even the inexpressive fioriture would sound less preposterous in the language of their origin with which they do not seem so out of keeping.

Mandane's splendid aria with trumpet obbligato, "The soldier tired of war's alarms", once the delight of all agile sopranos, has now disappeared from the concert repertory. It was last sung at Queen's Hall by Miss Ada Forest in 1910, to mark the bicentenary of the composer's birth. This was scarcely an adequate recognition of the anniversary, but it was all there was, and as far as it went it proved most stimulating. Would a revival of the famous aria, after the lapse of a quarter of a century, arouse the same degree of enthusiasm? We are inclined to think it might.

Chapter XI

THE FAIRY PRINCE—DEATH AND COMMEMORATION

Encouraged by his triumph with *Artaxerxes*, Dr Arne made another setting of Metastasio's words. This time it was *Olimpiade* which he left in the original Italian; but, as we have already seen, it failed completely, owing to the introduction of the ballad style which appears to have given great offence to Dr Burney and others, who condemned it as being beneath the dignity of Italian Opera. *Olimpiade* was only twice performed at the Haymarket Theatre and is now lost. Arne wisely made no further attempts of this kind.

Another field for his activities was the Madrigal Club, which his friend William Mawhood had founded for the singing of ancient madrigals. The club was for both professional and amateur musicians, and its meeting was the occasion of marked conviviality which was not always restrained within the limits of decorum. For these meetings Arne composed a great number of Catches and Glees, and through his interest this style of composition became very fashionable. His own glee, "Come, Shepherds, we'll follow the hearse", was always sung at the meeting that immediately succeeded the death of a member of the club. After Arne's own death it was sung at a benefit concert given for his wife. We should imagine that the poor woman must have found this rather a melancholy pleasure.

Dr Arne took great trouble with these Catches and Glees. He insisted always on their being very carefully rehearsed, and we hear of his conducting public concerts of them at Ranelagh, Drury Lane and the theatre in the Haymarket. The habit of unaccompanied singing had evidently fallen into disuse, for it was found necessary to explain to the audience what was meant by a Catch and by a Glee, and Arne was at pains to inform it that these had been much in fashion in the time of Purcell. These performances recreated a taste for part-songs and madrigals, which have never again diminished in popularity, and thenceforward a perfect torrent of them has poured, and is even now pouring, from the pens of British composers, one of the most notable of whom was Sir Henry Bishop (1786–1855).

In 1769 David Garrick wrote an ode to celebrate the opening of the new theatre at Stratford-on-Avon for which Arne composed music; but Garrick gives Arne a very poor chance and the *Ode to Shakespeare* is rather disappointing. The poetry is weak, and the music though effective and tuneful only twice reaches any very high degree of inspiration. The air "Thou soft-flowing Avon" is one of the precious things that can never be too frequent even among the works of the great song-writers; and very beautiful is the final duet with its simple but engaging counterpoint and exhilarating rhythm.

THE FAIRY PRINCE

Of the choruses a short fugue still survives to remind us of Arne's skill in this style of composition.

After a prolonged contemplation of Arne's second-rate and rather meretricious productions, it is with real joy that we at last come upon something that reminds us of his early spring, that season of promise, which in his case was only to be in part fulfilled. We have seen that the three masques which formed the keystone of his reputation followed each other in quick succession. Thirty years elapsed before a fourth masque appeared, which was equal in interest to each of the other three. It was only a flash in the pan, a flame that blazed up once more before the fire was finally extinguished, but it was enough to reassure us of the power to charm that Arne still possessed if he cared to use it.

In 1771 an investiture of the Order of the Garter was held at Windsor. Among those invested was the Duke of York, the second son of George III, and it is evidently in honour of this event that George Colman the Elder adapted Ben Jonson's *Masque of Oberon* to suit the occasion and called it *The Fairy Prince*. Arne wrote the music and the masque was performed at Covent Garden Theatre.

It is remarkable that this work either failed to interest or escaped the notice of W. H. Cummings, who mentions it only in the catalogue of works at the end of his book, and there misnames it *The Fairy Princess*. This omission is a matter for wonder, because in it there is to be found all the old spirit that animated *Comus*; the spirit of youth and freshness, of sincerity and gladness. Once again we seem to hear the young Arne as he was in the days when he spoke so sweetly and so well; it is his own melodious voice practising the enchantments of long ago. The whole masque is a riot of high spirits, and though it is bristling with the most exacting coloratura passages, they are not, on this occasion, mere vocal pyrotechnics but an essential part of the songs in which they occur, and add greatly to their effect.

The scene is laid in a "wild country", presumably Windsor Great Park. At the opening of the masque, a satyr sings a lively tenor aria calling upon his companions to join in welcoming the Fairy Prince. At first he succeeds only in raising an echo. The result is a playful duet in which the echo repeats each phrase of the satyr, sometimes picking it up before it is finished, so that the two parts overlap with amusing effect.

Silenus then appears, and a baritone aria in gavotte time celebrates the praises of the Prince. The mirth grows high, and now three satyrs sing a merry song accompanied by bells and bassoons.

The wood nymphs enter on the scene: a soprano aria of magical beauty invokes the choir of birds to serenade the king and queen. The birds are heard twittering along in the strings, until the voice calls upon the nightingale, whereupon the flute joins in the musical rhapsody. One delicious phrase grows out of another and weaves a spell about us from which we are scarcely free when a second nymph entrances us with a still more excitable aria into

THE FAIRY PRINCE

which horns are introduced, and where the voice darts about in a frenzy of delight.

All this enchanting music has been working towards a supreme climax, and in a more solemn but no less exultant strain the two soprano voices proclaim the actual presence of Majesty; the whole chorus in five parts burst in with the words "God save the King" sung in massive blocks of sound which turn our thoughts again towards Handel. The duet goes on its way and is again interrupted by a still more emphatic outburst from the chorus. But the soloists are not yet satisfied: their song is raised once more and a brilliant vocal flourish leads up to the mighty shout with which the chorus hail the Sovereign and bring the act to a triumphant conclusion. The design of this finale takes us back to "Rule, Britannia!". The same plan of verse and chorus is used, and the effect is achieved by the employment of the same method rather more fully developed.

It is all a very pretty compliment to the young king, George III, and it is some satisfaction to think that the tribute was not misdirected, for he, of all the German princes who have sat upon the throne of England, was the most deserving of the nation's respect, and the most ardent lover of music.

There are still delightful things to be heard in the remaining two acts of the masque, but as usual the music of the final chorus is missing and the work is therefore incomplete.

In *The Fairy Prince* free use is made of orchestral

colour, and besides the still unfamiliar clarinets, we find independent parts for flute, hautbois, bassoons, trumpets and horns, and even for carillon and timbrel. There is a suite of dances for the nymphs and satyrs, and two short processional marches scored for trumpets only. The slow movement of the overture is a graceful dance measure, one of the loveliest of its kind.

A great feature of this masque was evidently the scenery, for the names of the scene painters are given as Messrs Cipriani, Dall and Richards. These gentlemen must have found ample scope for their talent, for on one occasion a rock opens and discovers nothing less than the west front of St George's Chapel, brilliantly decorated. Again the scene opens and discovers a vision of the inside of the chapel "with the original knights in their several stalls". Later we are regaled with a tableau of the Battle of Crécy, and finally the scene changes to the "Inside of St George's Hall with the throne, tables, etc., as at the installation".

The musical style of *The Fairy Prince* differs from *Comus* in that the Handelian idiom is no longer so apparent, but neither is there any trace or taint of the Italian manner of *Artaxerxes*. The character of the writing is individual, free from affectation or sham emotion of any kind. It is Arne in a manner entirely his own, and one of the most delightful things he ever did.

There were to be no more such delights. This is the latest work that deserves more than a passing mention. The remaining years of Arne's life were taken up with the production of a few more farcical comedies, whose titles alone show us of what material they are composed: *The Cooper, Squire Badger, Achilles in Petticoats, Phoebe at Court,* all proclaim their style by their nomenclature: there are in each one of these a few tuneful little ditties that might help to cheer us on a rainy day, but nothing that we have not already discovered in *Thomas and Sally* and *Love in a Village. May-Day* with words by Garrick has several very charming songs, but the plot is tiresome, and would make poor entertainment on the stage.

In 1777 Dr Arne became very ill, and though his health improved again, the improvement was not maintained and at eight o'clock in the evening of March 5th, 1778, he died of a spasm in his lungs. There are two different accounts of his passing. The one from his friend Vernon, the tenor, is to the effect that he was himself talking to the doctor "who suffered much from exhaustion, and when attempting to illustrate what he had advanced, he in a very feeble and tremulous voice sung part of an air, during which he became progressively more faint until he breathed his last". This account would seem to be correct, for Vernon was an eyewitness of the scene and gave this report the following morning to the company who were assembled at the theatre.

The other description says that Arne had originally been instructed in the principles of the Romish Church, but these he had wholly neglected as inconsistent with a life of ease and gallantry in which he had indulged to the fullest extent of his purse and constitution. In his last stage the dormant seeds of early maxims revived in his bosom too strong to be checked. A priest was sent for and he was soon awed into a state of submissive repentance. About an hour before his death he sang a Hallelujah calculated, as it were, to usher him into the other world. This second narration is no doubt partly true; there is nothing in it that conflicts with the first, but the story is too fancifully told, and too much reliance should not be placed upon it.

Mrs Barthelemon relates that Arne died a sincere penitent and a firm Catholic, nor is there any reason whatever to doubt that he did so. If ever he had discontinued the practice of his religion it is most probable that he returned to it when he became reconciled to his wife, and did not wait until his dying moments. But there is no need to assume that even in the midst of a life of dissipation he neglected every act of worship, and we are expressly told that he attended the services at the Sardinian Chapel in Oxford Road.

At the time of his death Arne's reputation among his contemporaries had fallen somewhat from its high estate, and in spite of the immense popularity of *Artaxerxes* he had never recovered the position in the musical world which he had held in early life. This decline was to a large extent due to his private character. Garrick had sickened of him; Hawkins ignores him; Churchill, though not himself one who

THE FAIRY PRINCE

could afford to throw stones at any man, reviles him; and Burney, while conscious of his great merit, records his failings with justifiable severity. When he died there was no question of a great personality being removed; we hear of no solemn funeral, no universal mourning as in the case of Handel, not even a conventional ode to celebrate in extravagant terms the laurels he had once so fairly worn. A prominent figure had passed from the theatre, but the world in general heeded it not. Nevertheless, Arne had his champions, and of these none was more loyal nor louder in his praises than Charles Dibdin who, quite apart from his distinguished theatrical career, was soon to become the unofficial composer to the British Navy, his nautical ballads having been sung in every gun room of the Fleet. Arne had been kind to Dibdin by helping him over a difficult stile at the outset of his career, and the latter proclaimed his gratitude ever after in expressions of the wildest hyperbole. He could not say enough for his benefactor: *Artaxerxes* is referred to as "a great and magnificent composition than which, perhaps, no human attempt ever embraced wider perfection".

When Dibdin became co-director of a theatre he wished to bring forward a commemoration of Arne on a grand scale.

"I had supposed", he says, "a magnificent domain prepared for the reception of a nabob, and that some splendid festival should be given to circulate his popularity. It was suggested that the nabob would immortalise himself by rescuing the memory of some man of transcendent genius from oblivion, and perpetuating his fame by a noble and appropriate monument. The object recommended was, of course, to have been Arne. The entertainments were to have been of various descriptions, and the whole music selected from the works of the great musician whose friendship I once had the happiness to possess."

He wished also to erect a monument to Arne's memory, saying that he knew not of a greater national disgrace than that the remains of Arne who was, perhaps, take him all in all, the greatest composer that ever lived, should lie mouldering in obscurity. Furthermore, he tells us that at the time of Arne music was in its highest state of perfection in this country, and "scarcely had we lost Arne when Irish jigs usurped the musical domain. These having had their day, it was difficult to find a substitute, and now music is decidedly nowhere. Suppose then we were, by way of a change, to turn our thoughts to Arne again. Suppose the managers were to compile an entertainment from his works, and fairly give him the profits of his three nights, to erect a monument to him."

Without sharing Dibdin's limitless admiration, we cannot help being attracted by his wholehearted enthusiasm and loyalty, and it is sad to reflect that his noble endeavours to perpetuate Arne's fame were thwarted by the selfishness and avarice of his colleagues.

When the generation that had known Dr Arne

THE FAIRY PRINCE

personally had passed away and his delinquencies were forgotten, his fame as a musician rose again. An English school of quite competent song-writers, who all took their cue from him, carried on a national tradition, each producing a few really delightful songs, and thus helping to restrain the course that English music was taking towards its nadir; but these were not men of genius, and the distance that separates Storace, Shield, Linley, Horn, Hook and Bishop from Arne, Boyce and Greene is almost as extensive as that which divides these from Handel.

Dr Arne was *par excellence* the musician of Covent Garden as Purcell had been of Westminster. All the most important events of his life took place in that district, and most of his principal works were composed for its theatre. He was born in King Street, baptised and buried in St Paul's Church, lived in Bow Street, and, except for the few years spent in Ireland, his entire life was passed within the parish bounds. Now he is commemorated by a dingy little turning out of Long Acre that bears his name,* and a marble tablet, on which are inscribed the opening bars of "Rule, Britannia!", has been placed over his tomb in the church. On the occasion of the bi-centenary of his birth there was the intention to erect a memorial window; but not enough money was forthcoming, so this second attempt to raise a monument to Dr Arne failed as did the first. The third was more successful. The memorial tablet was unveiled

* This seems quite lately to have disappeared.

by Sir Frederick Bridge, the organist of Westminster Abbey, after which a curtain was drawn across the Sanctuary so that the congregation might forget that they were in church, and a most surprising collection of Arne's songs was sung. "When forced from dear Hebe to go" sounded strangely out of place.

In December 1930 another commemoration concert in the church was conducted on less incongruous lines. The programme included the motet *Libera me, Domine,* and some sacred or semi-sacred arias, besides fine examples of his instrumental music. The famous passage from Ecclesiasticus xliv was read and the concert concluded with a prayer for the composer.

Covent Garden still has its church and its theatre. Though Inigo Jones's St Paul's was burnt down in 1795, it was rebuilt on exactly the same plan; as long as it stands the memorial tablet will commemorate the great musician, and we may hope that from time to time his music may be performed within its walls. But the old theatre is gone, and of all the hordes of people who gravitate season after season towards the new Opera House with the name of the newest Italian tenor or German prima donna on their tongues, and who can talk fashionably of the latest operatic sensation, it is fairly safe to assert that not one ever gives a passing thought to the English master of song, who was the glory of Covent Garden during its great epoch, and that only a very small proportion of them have even heard his name.

THE FAIRY PRINCE

We are told that Arne was an ugly man, and the best authenticated portraits of him confirm this impression. The well-known print by Bartolozzi which is something of a caricature represents the composer in full dress with a sword, standing at the organ and playing "Rule, Britannia!": this print bears a strong resemblance to another portrait done in the last decade of his life; and a well executed full-length figure in high relief adorns the south-east angle of the frieze round the Albert Memorial. From these sources we get the impression that Dr Arne was a man of slender build; the face lantern-jawed and hollow cheeked, with prominent eyes too close together, and a long and slightly aquiline nose. Reproduced in *Dr Arne and "Rule Britannia!"* is a portrait of a boy with a flute, said to be a painting of Arne by Gainsborough, but this it cannot be, as Arne was already seventeen when Gainsborough was born, and as the boy with a flute is clearly in Gainsborough's manner, the inference is that the painting is his, but that the boy is not Arne.

Chapter XII

JUDITH

The story of Dr Arne has been told and all his principal vocal works have been surveyed in the order in which they were produced. We have seen that by far the greater number of these were written for the theatre, but there were two great exceptions, and one of these may be considered worthy of a chapter to itself. Of the two oratorios *Judith* alone remains, but it affords sufficient evidence of what Arne might have done had he turned his attention more to the composition of sacred music. Only the arias were ever published, but the choruses are still to be seen in manuscript in the British Museum, and these are not only the most important part of the oratorio but the greatest music that ever came from his pen. It is doubtful whether any other English composer ever wrote more grandly or more vigorously, and it can be only because these choruses are unknown that Arne is denied a place among the hierarchy of great choral writers. He himself regarded *Judith* as his *chef d'œuvre*, and he must have approached its composition in a befitting spirit, for we read on the last page of his manuscript the words "Laus Deo".

It was not only the composer who had a high opinion of this work; the oratorio was generally admired for many years, and, pasted into the cover of the British Museum manuscript there is a quotation from the ever-zealous Dibdin to the effect that Dr Arne's "*Judith* is one of the noblest compositions that ever stampt fame on a musician".

Judith was brought out at Drury Lane Theatre in February 1761, and repeated twice in March of the same year, and again in the Lent of 1762. Two years later it was revived for charitable purposes at the chapel of the Lock Hospital in Grosvenor Place, and in 1769 it formed part of the Shakespeare Jubilee Festival and was sung in the church at Stratford-on-Avon. In 1773 a performance took place at Covent Garden when, for the first time in history, women took the place of boys in the chorus of an oratorio.

A perusal of this work will dispel once and for all any lingering hopes that might yet be entertained of sorting Arne's styles neatly and methodically into periods, for it is a complete jumble of them all. Many of the arias are marred by the tawdry ornaments that we find in *Artaxerxes*, and the trivialities of the ballad operas crop up again in others, yet nowhere is Handel's influence more apparent than in the superb choruses where he comes nearer to his great prototype than on any other occasion.

In *Judith* Arne discovers a strong dramatic sense both in his grasp of situation and in his setting of words. The music changes with the mood of the scene and the choruses are equally convincing in their expressions of lamentation, entreaty, wrath, or exultation.

The oratorio is worth describing in some detail. The libretto is again by Isaac Bickerstaffe. It opens with a chorus which feelingly bewails the miseries of Judaea and offers up a fervent prayer for help; this is followed by a dramatic aria where the voice and the oboe alternately express their despair over a rushing accompaniment of strings. In the second part of this song the rhythm changes and the strings in short, gasping phrases vividly portray the exhaustion expressed in the words. The contralto voice next exhorts the people to put their faith in Jehovah, in a beautiful aria of which the concluding bars are spoilt by a meaningless cadenza. The appeal would, however, appear to have had the desired effect, for the music now cheers up and there follows the enchanting soprano aria, "Wake, my harp", which has the additional attraction of a harp obbligato. Judith herself now comes on to the scene and determines to save her country; but unfortunately she apprises us of her laudable resolution in a flamboyant aria that foreshadows the most shameless extravagances of *Artaxerxes*, and we turn from this sorry exhibition in disgust. But we are very soon appeased, for the chorus are next heard in a simple and very characteristic melody, the pastoral nature of which is delightfully emphasised by the inclusion of flutes and horns. The aria "Remember what Jehovah swore" is something of a surprise coming from Dr Arne. It is a solemn, rather austere declamation which would be heard to most advantage sung by a more powerful voice than is usually re-

JUDITH

quired for his music. The ornate passage, taking the voice up to C in alt, rings true in this particular song. It is as though the singer wished the tremendous prophecy to penetrate to the farthest corners of the earth. The words, too, are fine and are given their full value, for the most emphatic phrases are left unaccompanied, and the final declaration that "Heaven and Earth shall pass away, but not His Sacred Word" is made with a decision that admits of no dispute. In the bass air, "Conquest is not to bestow", the composer is guilty of a breach of decorum. He uses a measure and almost the same notes that he has on several previous occasions taught us to associate with the drinking bowl. "By the gaily circling glass" and "Bacchus, god of mirth and wine" instantly occur to our minds; excellent good songs they are, but when we find the words

> But the pious and the just,
> Those who in Jehovah trust

set to almost identical music, we feel that there must be something wrong somewhere.

The act ends with the first and longest of the three great choruses. "Hear, angels" is a magnificent song of praise in which the angels and celestial choirs are exhorted to join. At one point of this chorus it must be admitted that the likeness to Handel is so close as to amount to plagiarism. The inspiration is obviously drawn from the chorus in *Samson*, "Fixed in his everlasting seat", but the model is a good one, and the end justifies the means and needs no apology. This chorus is scored for trumpets and horns besides oboes and strings; the voices are first heard in massive blocks of sound, and later break into a short fugal section which culminates in Handel's favourite device of making the basses sing a sturdy run passage, while the other voices and the orchestra have a single sharp chord in each bar. When this passage is repeated the run is in the treble, the excitement is intensified by the semiquavers in the violins, the voices are once more heard in block harmonies, and the mighty chorus is brought to a triumphant end.

Few of the arias in the second and third parts have any great attraction. "Vain is beauty's gaudy flower" delights by its sheer loveliness; "Hail, immortal Bacchus" is a fine specimen of a rollicking drinking song for the bass voice in the character of Holofernes, and is followed by a chorus on the same theme; a peculiarity of "No more the heathen shall blaspheme" is its accompaniment for two 'cellos and figured bass only, otherwise it is of no great interest, nor do the remaining half dozen songs call for special comment, save one alone, "Sleep, gentle cherub", which is not only the most beautiful aria in *Judith* but perhaps the most perfect that Arne ever wrote. It is of the same high quality as "Not on beds of fading flow'rs" and "There honour comes" and even surpasses them. It occurs in the tensest scene of the drama when Judith lulls Holofernes into false security and invokes Sleep to spread his wings over her victim's senses. It is a moment

4. From the song "Sleep, gentle Cherub" (*Judith*).

of real inspiration. The accompaniment is written for string quartet moving slowly in counterpoint against the voice. There follows a short lyrical chorus, "Prepare the genial bower", exquisitely lovely, a soft enchanting lay, if ever there was one, to which very alluring strain Holofernes is inveigled to his doom: we could almost envy him.

Timpani add to the excitement of the chorus "Rejoice, Judaea falls", which bursts upon us like a thunderstorm and is as quickly over. Two great choruses yet remain: "Who can Jehovah's wrath abide?" consists of a majestic grave, a virile fugue, and a dramatic section that gathers speed and becomes a presto as the panic-stricken host of the Assyrians are smitten by the might of Jehovah's arm. The final chorus of the oratorio, "Here, sons of Jacob, let us rest", is the last triumphant song of thanksgiving calling for no other comment than the composer's own "Laus Deo" which we read at the end of his score.

It would be interesting to see what would be the effect of these choruses on an audience who only know Arne through the Shakespeare songs. Some day perhaps the experiment will be made, and who knows whether some enthusiast will not again be found exclaiming in the words of Charles Dibdin: "Judith is one of the noblest compositions that ever stampt fame on a musician"?

5. From the chorus "Here, sons of Jacob" (*Judith*).

6. From the chorus "Here, sons of Jacob" (*Judith*), continued.

Chapter XIII

REQUIESCAT—ET RESURGAT

Arne, we have seen, was a Roman Catholic and worshipped at the Sardinian Chapel in Oxford Road. He would not, therefore, have been likely to have set the canticles of the Anglican Liturgy nor to have written anthems for the Protestant Church as did Purcell, Boyce and Greene; but it is scarcely probable that with his genius for choral composition he did not contribute to the services of his own Church; yet only two examples of liturgical music still exist, both of which are in manuscript in the British Museum.* The first, an *O Salutaris Hostia* in four parts, is probably nothing more than a short exercise in counterpoint, in imitation of the music of an earlier date; the second, *Libera me, Domine*, in five parts, is one of the composer's most important works. It is called in the manuscript a dirge.

This dirge is curiously unlike anything we know of Arne's, unless we see in it faint traces of the dirge in

* It has been brought to my notice that one of the choristers of the Sardinian Chapel collected several of Arne's manuscripts and took them to Rome for presentation to Henry Stuart, Cardinal of York, the younger brother of Prince Charles Edward. The Cardinal was a great admirer of Arne's music, and at his death the MSS. were added to the Vatican Library. A portion of a Mass has recently been copied and sung in a church in Newcastle-on-Tyne. H.L.

Romeo and Juliet, and not one of his many styles with which we are familiar is apparent in it. It is reasonable, therefore, to suppose that in writing for the Church Arne adopted a completely different method, as far removed as possible from any English influence, and essentially Latin in style and temper.

The manuscript of this work is not in Arne's own handwriting, but in that of a copyist, and has many errors. It was presented to the Musical Antiquarian Society by Vincent Novello, whose father sang the bass part, and who was himself a chorister in the Sardinian Chapel. Special attention has been paid to it by Dr Cummings in his *Dr Arne and "Rule, Britannia!"*, and it is to him that we owe its discovery.

It appears to have been performed only on the occasion for which it was expressly composed, the funeral of one Francis Pemberton, a friend of Dr Arne, and it was never printed. Thanks, however, to the reference in Dr Cummings's book, copies have been made and performances given by the British Broadcasting Corporation, and the Oriana Madrigal Society: it was also sung by five solo voices at the memorial concert to Dr Arne at St Paul's, Covent Garden, in 1930. On each occasion it was received with the greatest favour, and the broadcast performance has been twice repeated.

The dirge is in five sections, of which the first is the longest. This is a solemn and very impressive setting for chorus of the words "Libera me, Domine, de morte aeterna". It is followed by a short bass

7. From the dirge "*Libera me*"

8. From the dirge "*Libera me*", continued.

solo, stern and weighty, "Tremens factus sum", which modulates from the key of A minor to the relative major, and when this has been established there are eight bars of chorus sung pianissimo. This little choral episode is one of the most telling moments of the whole work. The "Dies irae" is another short solo for tenor in six-four time, rounded off as before by a few bars of chorus.

To the soprano soloist has been left the first note of consolation which we are permitted to hear. "Requiem aeternam" is a separate aria, of greater length than either of the other two, and the point up to which the foregoing sections have been leading. The major key has a most touching effect. It is as though a merciful hand were laid upon us, and our tears wiped away. Italian divisions are made use of, but are not inappropriate and do not distract us. This aria is in E major, and for the final "Requiescat in pace" the chorus enter unexpectedly in the key of G.* There are only eleven bars of this "Requiescat", and getting ever softer the music fades away, and the dirge is finished.

With this beautiful little work of genuine affection for his departed friend, and with his "Requiescat in pace" still in our minds, we will bring the account

---

* This change is so abrupt that it has been suggested that something may be missing, or that Arne supplied some chords at the organ which were never written down. I do not myself subscribe to this opinion, for though the effect is unusual in music of this period, it is strangely beautiful and, I think, deliberate. H.L.

of Arne's vocal music to an end, that branch of the art wherein he most excelled, and turn our attention to his compositions for instruments. These consist of six concertos for organ or harpsichord; eight overtures for hautbois and strings; seven sonatas for two violins and figured bass; and eight lessons for the harpsichord. Of these only the harpsichord lessons are published or played with any frequency.

There is considerable variety in these lessons, and no two of them are on the same pattern. They consist of vigorous toccatas, lively dance tunes, and wistful little airs: one in D minor is of sterner stuff and contains a fine fugue. The last lesson is a set of rather poor variations on a minuet of Rameau.

Of the overtures or symphonies, the last two are also the overtures to *Comus* and *The Judgment of Paris*. The former begins with a maestoso of great authority which at once arrests our attention and commands our respect. There is nothing feeble here; nor is there in the fugue, which again impresses us by its virility. The overture to *The Judgment of Paris* starts with a largo and a fugue which are followed by a minuet and a spirited gigue for strings. Four of these overtures open with fast movements and each has three movements. In the introductory movement to No. 2 in A major the violins arouse our excitement by some remarkable scale passages which, each time they occur, lead up to two emphatic chords. The 6th in B flat is a masterly achievement consisting of a slow introduction, a fugue of two subjects, and a most delightful gavotte. This overture, very well suited to small orchestras, has been broadcast: it has also been played at several concerts and received with acclamation, but as it is still unpublished and only one set of parts is available, the supply has not been equal to the demand, or it would have been heard more often. The three dances from *Comus* which have been recently published have proved most popular and useful. They are very good examples of Arne's work for orchestra: particularly beautiful is the one in slow time, where the strings are joined by the flute.

The trio-sonatas should always be played with a 'cello in conjunction with the continuo. It is a pity that this combination of instruments has gone out of fashion, for some of the best chamber music has been written for this ensemble, and among the many hundreds of these sonatas turned out between 1700 and 1750 Arne's stand extremely high. Of the seven which he wrote, the first in A is the most important. It is unusually long, being in five movements all of which are admirable: an andante; a fugue; a short grave leading into a scuttling vivace; and a minuet with trio which, lovely as it is the first time through, is yet more so when the minuet is repeated with pizzicato 'cello passages. This sonata has been published in Germany. The sonatas in E flat and E minor are both excellent, and one in F minor is remarkable for its austerity and the mournful beauty of its first quick movement.

In 1934 two overtures and a group of songs were performed at one of the Courtauld-Sargent concerts at Queen's Hall: the orchestra was the Philharmonic, the conductor George Szell of Prague: this caused considerable stir. The first thing that happened was that Dr Arne was sent from a "Press Cutting agency" the following letter, which has been carefully preserved, envelope and all:

Sir—May we supply you with press cuttings relating to yourself and your public appearances from the English and Colonial Press? We have a large theatrical, musical, and kinematograph department and can guarantee a thorough supply of notices.

We enclose numbered terms. Yearly contracts can be made with clients requiring an unlimited number of cuttings.

Trusting to be favoured with a trial order,
We are etc.

Dr Arne was no longer able to avail himself of this means of watching the progress of his fame, but some of us who were more fortunate were gratified to read many tributes to him in the Press, of which the following are a representative selection:

The Sunday Times: "Mr Szell had the enterprise to turn to our own Dr Arne for other treasures which should not be forgotten. All this was captivating, melodious, lightsome music."

The Daily Mail: "There was a great English composer represented, Dr Arne. Two overtures were played and proved that their neglect does us little credit. Even better were two of his songs."

The Morning Post: "Why has the delicious overture

to *The Judgment of Paris* been overlooked? Why have the charming *Masque of Alfred* songs been so neglected? No music could be more English in its robust vitality, its freshness, and its charm. This happy resuscitation is a reason for our gratitude."

The Star: "Our own Arne provided a couple of overtures and three charming songs. This item certainly pleased the large audience, if applause is any criterion."

For at least one evening Arne had come into his own: the performers and the public with one accord conspired to praise him, which has been invariably the case in smaller concerts whenever in recent years a performance of any of his music has been arranged. This is satisfactory as far as it goes, but it does not go very far. By private enterprise something can be done to bring to the notice of a small public some special work that can be sung without too much expense or difficulty, but once the tumult and the shouting have died little has been accomplished if the music remains unpublished. Boyce and Arne are peculiar sufferers in this sort; but though Boyce's fine vocal works remain unknown, his symphonies have been re-edited and are rapidly becoming familiar, whereas in the case of Arne not one single work of primary importance is in print or available in its entirety for the theatre or the concert hall. The statement of this discreditable fact cannot be over-emphasised. *Comus* has been required for performance both on the Continent and in the United States, but no score being obtainable the project has had to be abandoned in each case; and the orchestral overtures have on more than one occasion suffered the same fate. When the publishers can be prevailed upon to do their share, the musicians and the audience will be ready. That a revival and reinstatement of Dr Arne's music will some day occur can be confidently expected. It is greatly to be hoped that they will come soon, for though he was not one of the prophets or evangelists destined, as were Handel and Bach, to make the world better and wiser, he was yet richly endowed with powers for making it happier and more gracious, which we, who live in an age less contented and far less polished than his, can ill afford to despise.

APPENDIX A

EXTANT WORKS OF ARNE

In the MS. Dept. of the British Museum are to be found:

Judith: an oratorio (autograph score).
Finale of *The Judgment of Paris*; only a fragment (autograph).
"God bless our noble king", arranged by Arne for trio and three-part chorus, two horns and viola, 1745 (autograph).
Rosamond: an opera (six songs and three duets).
The Tempest ("Come unto these yellow sands" and the masque).
Motet: *Libera me, Domine* (for soloists and five-part chorus and organ).
Motet: *O Salutaris Hostia* (unaccompanied four-part chorus).

The following works of Dr Arne are in the British Museum catalogue: the dates of their production are in brackets.

VOCAL MUSIC

Rosamond: "Rise glory" and "Was ever nymph like Rosamond?" (1733).
Tom Thumb: overture and one song (1733).
The fall of Phaeton: "O come, O come my dearest" (1736).
Comus (1738).
An Hospital for fools (1739).
The Judgment of Paris (1740).

APPENDIX A

The Masque of Alfred (1740).
Music in *As You Like It* (1740).
Songs in *Twelfth Night* (1741).
The Blind Beggar of Bethnal Green (1741).
Songs in *The Merchant of Venice* (1742).
Britannia: a masque (1743).
Abel: an oratorio ("Hymn of Eve") (1744).
Songs in *The Tempest* (1746).
Love's Labour's Lost ("When icicles hang by the wall") (1747).
Dirge in *Romeo and Juliet* (1750).
Harlequin Sorcerer: duet (1752).
Thomas and Sally (1760).
Judith: an oratorio (1761).
Eliza: an opera (1755).
Artaxerxes: an opera (1762).
Love in a Village: a ballad opera (1762).
The Guardian Outwitted: comic opera (1764).
Ode to Shakespeare (1769).
The Jovial Crew (1769).
Additions to *King Arthur* of Purcell (1770).
The Ladies' Frolic (1770).
The Fairy Prince: a masque (1771).
The Cooper: a comic opera (1772).
Music in Mason's *Elfrida* (1772).
Achilles in Petticoats: a comic opera (1773).
Duet in *The Rival Queens* (1774).
May-Day: a comic opera (1776).
Six Cantatas for voice and instruments.

Separate songs in various collections.

The Agreeable Musical Choice.
Lyric Harmony.

APPENDIX A

Vocal Melody.
The Vocal Grove.

INSTRUMENTAL MUSIC

Six concertos for keyboard instrument with orchestra.
Eight overtures for orchestra.
Eight lessons or sonatas for harpsichord.
Seven sonatas for two violins and figured bass.

Early Editions of Dr Arne's principal works are sometimes obtainable from second-hand music shops: most of these with orchestral parts in manuscript are also in the possession of the author who is always willing to lend them for performance.

APPENDIX B

MODERN EDITIONS OF ARNE'S WORKS

The following works are obtainable at the present time, either separately or in various collections of songs:

VOCAL MUSIC

ORATORIOS

THE DEATH OF ABEL
"Hymn of Eve"

JUDITH
"Sleep, gentle Cherub." (Joseph Williams.)
Chorus: "Here, sons of Jacob, let us rest." (O.U.P.)

OPERAS AND MASQUES

ROSAMOND
"Was ever nymph like Rosamund?" (Augener.)

COMUS
"Now Phoebus sinketh in the west." (Augener.)
"By dimpled brook." (Curwen.)
"How gentle was my Damon's air." (Augener.)
"Would you taste the noontide air?" (Stainer and Bell.)
"Come, bid adieu to fear." (Stainer and Bell.)
"Fame's an echo." (Joseph Williams.)
"Not on beds of fading flow'rs." (Joseph Williams.)

THE JUDGMENT OF PARIS
"O, ravishing delight." (Novello.)
"Fear not, mortal." (Stainer and Bell.)

APPENDIX B

"Gentle swain." (Novello.)
"Stay, lovely youth." (Stainer and Bell.)

ALFRED

"Guardian angels." (Stainer and Bell.)
"O Peace, thou fairest child." (Curwen.)
"Vengeance, O come inspire me." (Joseph Williams.)
"Tho' storms awhile the sun obscure." (Augener.)
"Come, calm content." (Augener.)
"Arise, sweet messenger of morn." (Joseph Williams.)
"Rule, Britannia!" (Augener.)

LOVE IN A VILLAGE (Boosey.)

"Gentle youth."
"The traveller benighted."
Duet: "All I wish."
Trio: "Well, come, let us hear."

ELIZA

"Oh for music's pleasing strains." (Stainer and Bell.)

THOMAS AND SALLY

"All ye who would wish to succeed." (Augener.)
"When I was a young one." (Augener.)
"Sure, Sally is the loveliest lass." (Augener.)
"The echoing horn." (Augener.)

SHAKESPEARE SONGS

"Where the bee sucks." (Augener.)
"Blow, blow, thou winter wind." (Augener.)
"Under the greenwood tree." (Augener.)

"Come away, Death." (Novello.)
"Sigh no more, ladies." (Augener.)
"When daisies pied." (Augener.)
"When icicles hang by the wall." (Augener.)

ARTAXERXES

"The soldier tired of war's alarms." (Novello.)
Duet: "For thee I live, my dearest." (Augener.)
"Water parted from the sea." (Augener.)

ODE TO SHAKESPEARE

"Thou soft-flowing Avon." (Novello.)

SONGS

"The Confession." (Joseph Williams.)
"O come, O come, my dearest." (Joseph Williams.)
"The honest lover." (Augener.)
"Lotharia." (Joseph Williams.)
"My Grandmother's cot." (Joseph Williams.)
"Why so pale and wan, fond lover?" (Joseph Williams.)
"Still to be neat." (Joseph Williams.)
"Come, Rosalind, Oh, come and see." (Joseph Williams.)
"Polly Willis." (Curwen.)
"My banks they are furnished with bees." (Augener.)
"Bacchus, god of mirth and wine." (Novello.)
"When forced from dear Hebe to go." (Augener.)
"Fresh and strong the breeze is blowing." (Novello.)
"When youth's sprightly flood." (Novello.)
"Despairing beside a clear stream." (Novello.)
"The sycamore shade." (Novello.)

APPENDIX B 113

"The topsails shiver in the wind." (Novello.)
"The Shepherd." (Novello.)
"The miller of Mansfield." (Novello.)
"My dog and my gun." (Augener.)
"The retort." (Augener.)
"Strephon of the Mill." (Augener.)
"The arch denial." (Augener.)
"Decrepit winter limps away." (Augener.)
"Sweet Nan of the vale." (Augener.)
"Ye fair, possessed of every charm." (Augener.)
"The plague of love." (Edited by Lane Wilson.)
"Under the rose." (Augener.)
"Go, lovely rose." (Augener.)
"Delia." (Augener.)
"The kind inconstant." (Augener.)
"The complaint." (Augener.)
"Come, Mira." (Augener.)

INSTRUMENTAL WORKS

Overture No. 4 in F. (Augener.)
Dances from *Comus*. (O.U.P.)
Sonata for two violins and bass in A. (Breitkopf and Härtel.)
Sonata for two violins and bass in E minor. (Novello.)
Lessons for the harpsichord. (Augener.)

BIBLIOGRAPHY

Dr Arne and "Rule, Britannia!" W. H. Cummings (1912).

Life and Works of Dr Arne. B. H. Horner (1893).

Burney's *History of Music* (1782-9).

Memoirs of the Musical Drama. George Hogarth (1838).

Abraham Rees's Cyclopaedia, vol. 2 (1819).

Temple Bar, vol. 117 (1899).

Mrs Delaney: *Autobiography and Correspondence*, ed. Lady Llanover (1861).

Charles Dibdin: *Autobiography* (1803).

A History of Music in England. Ernest Walker (1924).

Stage Favourites of the Eighteenth Century. Lewis Melville (1928).

Grove's Dictionary of Music.

Dictionary of National Biography.

Charles Churchill's Poetical Works (1804).

Musical Anecdotes. Frederick Crowest (1878).

INDEX

Achilles in Petticoats, 81
Acis and Galatea, 13, 53
Addison, 17, 39
Aeschylus, 16
Aix-la-Chapelle, 49
Albert Memorial, 87
Alexander's Feast, 38
Alfred, Masque of, 26–32, 38, 39, 55, 65, 105
Allegro, 37, 49
"All I wish", 69
"Angels ever bright and fair", 27
Anne, Queen, 12
Antonio, 28
"Arise, sweet messenger", 27
Arne, Edward, 13
Arne, Michael (composer's brother), 17
Arne, Michael (composer's son), 14, 50, 55, 62
Arne, Mrs, 17, 18, 36, 37, 38, 39, 52, 53–63
Arne, Susannah, *see* Cibber, Mrs
Arne, Thomas, sen., 12
Arne, Thomas Augustine, and the photographer, 4; at Eton, 5; success in his lifetime, 6; instructs Burney, 9; birth, 12; studies law, 17; first composition, 17; marries, 17; masques, 19–32; goes to Dublin, 35; acts in Shakespeare's *Henry IV*, 39; appointed to Drury Lane, 39; goes to Dublin, 53; judges between two singers, 54; leaves his wife, 55; deterioration in character, 58; reconciliation with his wife, 61; death, 81; Commemoration Concerts, 85, 86; personal appearance, 87; instrumental music, 102; Courtauld-Sargent Concert, 103
Artaxerxes, 11, 45, 56, 64, 65, 71–75, 80, 82, 83, 89, 90
As You Like It, 33
Augusta, Princess, 26
Austria, 1

"Bacchus, god of mirth and wine", 91
Bach, 106
Barnes, James, 13
Bartolozzi, 87
Beard, 7, 20, 40, 49, 67, 71
Beggar's Opera, 4, 48
"Believe me, dear aunt", 70
Bellini, 73
Bickerstaffe, 67, 68, 69, 90
Bishop, 76, 85
Blake, 6 n.
"Blow, blow, thou winter wind", 33
Boyce, 3, 85, 97, 105
Brandenburg Concertos, 47
Brent, Charlotte, 45, 53, 54, 67, 71, 72, 74
Bridge, Sir F., 86
British Broadcasting Corporation, 98
British Museum, 88, 89, 97
British Navy, 83

INDEX

Burney, Dr Charles, 9–11, 18, 30, 40, 42, 45, 50, 58, 63, 64, 72, 75, 83
Burney, Fanny, 45
"By dimpled brook", 22

"*Calypso and Telemachus*", 69
Champness, 59
Chelsea Hospital, 49
Churchill, 7, 72, 73, 82
Cibber, Colley, 7
Cibber, Mrs, 7, 14–16, 35, 36, 40
Cibber, Theophilus, 15
Cipriani, 80
Clive, Kitty, 7, 52, 53
Cliveden, 26, 28, 30, 31
Collins, 26, 27
Colman, George, 77
"Come away, Death", 34
"Come if you dare", 59
"Come, shepherds, we'll follow the hearse", 75
Comus, 4, 7, 8, 10, 11, 20–23, 35, 37, 38, 42, 43, 50, 54, 65, 66, 77, 80, 102, 103, 105
Concerti Grossi, 47
"Conquest is not to bestow", 91
Cooper, The, 81
Crécy, Battle of, 80
'Crown and Cushion", 12
Cummings, W. H., 77, 98

Dall, 80
Dalton, Dr John, 20
"Damon and Florella", 53
D'Arblay, Mme, *see* Burney, Fanny
Death of Abel, The, 38
Delaney, Dr, 7
Delaney, Mrs, 55, 56
Denmark, 32 n.
Devonshire, Duke of, 36

Dibdin, Charles, 35, 83, 84, 89, 94
Dido and Aeneas, 69
"Dies Irae", 101
Donizetti, 73
Dryden, 59
Dublin, 7, 35–39, 44, 53, 54, 55
Duke of York, 77

Edinburgh, 44, 53
Elijah, 61
Eliza, 54, 65, 70, 71 n.
Esther, 53
Eton, 5
Evelina, 46

Fairy Prince, The, 19, 65, 77–80
Farquhar, 67
"Fear not, mortal", 25
Festing, Michael, 12, 17, 49
Fétis, 10
Firework Music, 49
"Fixed in his everlasting seat", 91
Forest Ada, 74
"From the dawn of early morning", 27

Gainsborough, 87
Galliards, 69
Garrick, 7, 15, 35, 36, 58, 59, 60, 82
Gay, 4
"Gentle swain", 25
George II, 4, 40, 48
George III, 1, 77, 79
Gilbert and Sullivan, 66
"God save our noble King", 40
"Grant me, ye Powers", 68
Greene, 3, 85, 97
Greville, Fulk, 9
"Guardian Angels", 27

INDEX

"Hail, immortal Bacchus", 92
Hallelujah, 82
Handel, 1–3, 5, 6, 7, 16, 30, 35, 36, 37, 42, 43, 47–50, 54, 60, 79, 83, 85, 89, 91, 106
Harlequin Sorcerer, 53
Harpsichord Lessons, 103
Hawkins, 45, 82
Haydn, 1
"Hear, Angels", 91
Henry IV, Pt II, 39
Henry VI, 6
"Here, sons of Jacob", 94
"He was despised", 16
Hogarth, 47
Hook, 85
Horn, 85
"How gentle was my Damon's air", 22
"How sleep the brave", 26
Huggins, John, 13
Hullah, John, 52
"Hymn of Eve", 39

Isaiah, 16

Jeune Sage et le Vieux Fou, Le, 66
Jones, Inigo, 86
Jonson, Ben, 77
Judas Maccabaeus, 23 n.
Judgment of Paris, 22–5, 26, 28, 38, 39, 44, 64, 102, 105
Judith, 19, 44, 65, 88–94

Keats, 8
King Arthur, 59, 60

Lampe, Mrs, 53
Largo, 30
La Serva Padrona, 66
"Lass with a delicate air", 55
Laus Deo, 88, 94

Le Barberini, 30
"Let not a moon-born elf", 59
Libera me, Domine, 19, 86, 97, 98
"Lilliburlero", 28
Linley, 85
Lock Hospital, 89
London Bridge, 49
Long Acre, 85
"Lotharia", 51
Love in a Village, 51, 69, 70, 81
Love's Labour's Lost, 33, 53
Lowe, 30, 50

Madrigal Club, 75
Mallet, David, 26
"Marseillaise", 28
Mary-le-bone, 46
Mawhood, 75
May-Day, 66, 81
Méhal, 66
Mendelssohn, 2, 61
Merchant of Venice, 33
Messiah, 7, 35, 36
Metastasio, 11, 66, 71, 75
Milton, 16, 20
Mozart, 50, 68
Much Ado About Nothing, 53
"My heart ever faithful", 27

"Nature framed thee", 23
"*Nightingale, The*", 60
"No more the heathen", 92
"Not on beds", 20, 92
Novello, Vincent, 98
Novello's, 49 n.
"Now Phoebus sinketh in the west", 22

Ode in honour of Great Britain, see "Rule, Britannia!"
Ode to Shakespeare, 76
Olimpiade, 10, 66, 75

118 INDEX

"Ombra mai fu", 30
"O Peace, thou fairest child", 27
Operas, 64
Oratorios, 38, 88
"O ravishing delight", 23
"O rest in the Lord", 61
Oriana Madrigal Society, 98
O Salutaris Hostia, 97, 107
Overtures, 103
Oxford, 64

Parry, Hubert, 6
Pemberton, Francis, 98
Pepusch, 64
Perelli, 71, 72
Pergolesi, 66
Phoebe at Court, 81
"Polly Willis", 51
Portia, 28
"Prepare the genial bower", 94
Prince of Wales, 26, 30
Purcell, 6, 10, 11, 20, 42, 59, 60, 69, 76, 85, 97

Queen's Hall, 74, 104
Quin, 7, 15, 36

Rameau, 102
Ranelagh, 45, 49, 76
"Rejoice, Judaea falls", 94
"Remember what Jehovah swore", 90
"Requiem aeternam", 101
"Requiescat in pace", 101
"Return, O God", 16
Rheinhold, 40, 50
Richards, 80
Roderick Random, 8
Romeo and Juliet, 34, 53, 97
Rosamond, 17, 38, 54
Rosciad, The, 7, 72
Roubiliac, 49

"Rule, Britannia!", 4, 5, 23, 26–32, 79, 85, 87

"Safe beneath this lowly dwelling", 27
St George's Chapel, 80
St George's Hall, 80
St Martin's-in-the-Fields, 62
St Paul's, Covent Garden, 12, 85, 86, 98
Samson, 16, 91
Sardinian Chapel, 82, 97, 98
Senesino, 30
Serse, 30
Shakespeare, 33, 34, 35, 43, 76, 89, 94
Shenstone, 51
Sheridan, 67
She Stoops to Conquer, 8
Shield, 85
Shylock, 28
"Sleep, gentle Cherub", 92
Sloper, 15
Smollett, 8
"Soldier tired of war's alarms", 74
Solomon, 53
Squire Badger, 81
Stanford, 42
Storace, 85
Stuart, Charles Edward, 40
Stuart Henry, Cardinal of York, 97
"Sweet bird", 37
"Sweet valley", 27
Symphonies, 103
Szell, George, 104

Tempest, The, 33, 53, 54
Tenducci, 71, 72
"There honour comes", 27, 92
Thomas and Sally, 66–9, 71, 81

INDEX

Thomson, James, 26, 27
"Tremens factus sum", 101
Trio-sonatas, 103
Twelfth Night, 33
Tyers, 49

"Under the greenwood tree", 33

"Vain is beauty's gaudy flower", 92
Vauxhall Gardens, 10, 11, 45–51
Vernon, 81

"Wake, my harp", 90
Walpole, Horace, 49
Walpole, Robert, 48
Walpurgisnacht, 61
"Water parted from the sea", 8, 73

Weelkes, 60
"Well, come, let us hear", 69
Westminster, 85
Westminster Abbey, 1, 15, 86
Wheeler, Anne, 12
"When daisies pied", 33
"When forced from dear Hebe", 51, 86
"Where the bee sucks", 33, 53
"Who can Jehovah's wrath abide", 94
Windsor, 77
"Wise men flatt'ring", 23
"Would you taste the noontide air?", 8

Young, Cecilia, *see* Arne, Mrs
Young, Polly, 55, 61, 63, 82

Made in the USA
Monee, IL
03 May 2026